A Surface Creek Christmas

Winter Tales 1904–1910

Book 1 in the Surface Creek Life Series

A Surface Creek Christmas

Winter Tales 1904–1910

Book 1 in the Surface Creek Life Series

D.P. Benjamin

ELEVATION PRESS

A Surface Creek Christmas
By D.P. Benjamin

For more information, please see *About the Author* at the close of this book and visit benjaminauthor.com

Cover art and Christmas tree illustrations by Carol Ann Rasmussen.

Cover design and interior design and formatting by Donna Marie Woods Benjamin.

Elevation Press
P.O. Box 603
Cedaredge, CO 81413

Ordering information: Quantity sales. Special discounts are available on quantity purchases by book clubs, corporations, associations, and others. For details, contact the publisher at the address above.

ISBN 978-0-932624-13-0

1. Main category— [United States History] 2. Other categories—[Genealogy]—[Colorado] [Christmas]

ELEVATION PRESS
© 2022
Elevation Press
Cedaredge, Colorado
www.elevation-press-books.com

For information on services offered by Elevation Press, please see the final page of this book.

❧ A note about the book cover ❧

I am indebted to my colleague and neighbor, Carol Ann Rasmussen for permission to feature her enchanting artwork on the cover of *A Surface Creek Christmas.*

❧ Dedication ❧

This book is dedicated to the memory of Clyde W. and Alpha Brewer whose unwavering support for their community is forever enshrined in the rich and memorable pages of the *Surface Creek Champion.* And also to the Surface Creek Valley Historical Society for their tireless efforts to preserve local history.

❦ Foreword ❧

A Surface Creek Christmas
Winter Tales 1904–1910
Book 1 in the Surface Creek Life Series

This book highlights six years of historic holiday happenings as celebrated in Western Colorado. Gleaned from the pages of the popular weekly newspaper which once served the Surface Creek Valley, these tidbits take the reader on a nostalgic journey into the realm of Christmases past. Published from 1904–1943, the *Surface Creek Champion* newspaper faithfully reported the joys and tragedies, triumphs and foibles of a bygone era.

The popular weekly newspaper was first published by C.T. Rawalt and managed by Clyde W. Brewer, who ultimately took over editorial, proprietary, and publisher responsibilities beginning in June 1905. In naming their publication the *Champion,* its creators had in mind the championing of the Surface Creek Valley with its hardy people, unique communities, spectacular scenery, and vigorous enterprises of fruit, crops, and cattle.

The early days of newspaper work in the Surface Creek region relied on reports from amateur correspondents. As a result, facts were seldom verified and names may have been wrongly reported. Then too, before ink could be pressed to paper, everything was set in reverse and one letter at a time, using leaded type—a laborious process which sometimes led to inadvertent misspellings.

The oldest editions of the *Champion* conformed to a predictable pattern. The large sheets of coarse paper on which early newspapers were imprinted often arrived with interior pages already full of pre-printed stories. Many small papers were run by one or two dedicated souls and having two pages already filled made it far easier to gather enough local advertisements and local news to fill front and back pages. Interior pages featured general news from other states and nations as well as "canned" serialized stories, recipes, patented medicine advertisements, and other generic items.

To clarify my approach to this book, events attributed to Christmas of a given year reflect the contents of a series of weekly newspapers published throughout December of that year. For example, my "Christmas 1904" summary reflects the contents of *Champion* newspapers published on December 2, 9, 16, 23, and 30, 1904. This approach takes into account Christmas events which are predicted and captures follow-up stories published in the wake of holiday activities.

In my efforts to summarize the news of past Christmas seasons, I have endeavored to give the reader a tolerable flavor of the times. I have not included in my summation hundreds of brief stories about the comings and goings of local citizens—who left the Valley for a visit, who paid a visit to the Valley, who celebrated a birthday, etc. These seemingly mundane events were, naturally, of paramount interest to past readers. In fact, these single-sentence and very personal reports truly formed the lifeblood of the *Champion*. But including all these notices was simply impractical.

By the same token, in the interest of space, I have not included every birth announcement, wedding, or obituary which was published between 1904 and 1910. However, I have sprinkled a few such mentions throughout this book to give the reader a taste of these vital events.

I had originally intended for each book in this series to cover ten years, but the sheer volume of information, coupled with a decision to take on the challenging task of creating an index to aid the reader, obliged me to focus on a series of six-year slices.

A curious note: the reader will find that most proper names included in this volume appear with the person's first and middle initials followed by the last name, for example: C.W. Brewer. At one time, in written publications, those of a lower class had their first and middle names abbreviated under the mistaken assumption that it was presumptuous for a "common" person to be identified by a fulsome name. Thus, a servant or farmer or laborer whose given name was Alfred Bernard Smith was abbreviated to A.B. Smith. No such sinister intention caused early American newspapers to use initials in place of first and middle names. It seems such truncations were merely a way of saving space when the most important thing was to get the surname right.

From 1904 to 1910, the *Champion* literally grew with each edition. Beginning with four pages, the newspaper soon expanded to six and eight pages with one special holiday publication expanding to twelve. More pages meant more work for the newspaper's staff which, at most, appears to have included Clyde W. Brewer and perhaps three helpers—not counting his children who were recruited by their industrious father. But an expanded paper also meant more advertising revenue and, for readers, additional news and more features.

The *Champion's* growth also encompassed increasing sophistication. While local news continued to be scattered throughout the paper rather than gathered into discrete categories, there was some effort to cluster school and church and other like events into adjacent columns. Most significantly, by 1906, the rather unprofessional practice of placing advertisements on the front page had been discontinued in favor of showcasing prime stories and breaking news.

Clyde W. and his wife Alpha Brewer were larger than life characters whose tireless community spirit fashioned an enduring written history of the Surface Creek Valley. A substantial book could be written about each of the Brewers and, in fact, detailed accounts of both their lives have been compiled by family historians. I have not included comprehensive biographies in this book. For general biographies of Mr. and Mrs. Brewer, the reader is directed to Hazel Baker Austin's *Surface Creek Country: By a Native Daughter* which, along with other reference resources listed at the close of this book, is available for check-out at the Delta County Libraries. Some books may also be purchased at Cedaredge's Pioneer Town gift shop.

Ms. Austin is also the source of a succinct description of the region which comprises the Surface Creek Valley. Inasmuch as I can't say it any better, I have quoted her description and fashioned it into the lion's share of my introduction which follows.

This small book merely scratches the surface of a wealth of community history. Readers are invited and encouraged to view enlarged digital copies of the historic pages of the *Champion* newspaper for themselves. Instructions for accessing the full on-line collection can be found at the close of this book.

Sprinkled throughout this book, the reader will discover occasional author's notes which, I hope, will supply a measure of context and clarification. While certain idioms and references were readily understood by the *Champion's* original audience, some dated concepts may not resonate with modern readers. Where clarifications and explanations seem appropriate, I have attempted to provide context by inserting information gathered from sources outside the pages of the *Surface Creek Champion.*

A final note: I have endeavored to faithfully reproduce the substance and tone of vintage newspaper articles, sometimes rewording stories, but always striving to preserve the heart of matters which touched the lives of those no longer living. However, should the reader discover a particularly glaring error, please bring it to my attention using the address information on the copyright page and I will strive to correct the oversight in future editions.

—*D.P. Benjamin/November 19, 2022*

Books in the *Surface Creek Life* Series:

- **Book 1:** *A Surface Creek Christmas/Winter Tales 1904–1910*
- **Book 2:** *A Surface Creek Thaw/Spring Tales 1911–1917*
- **Book 3:** *A Surface Creek Solstice/Summer Tales 1918–1924*
- **Book 4:** *A Surface Creek Harvest/Autumn Tales 1925–1931*
- **Book 5:** *A Surface Creek Postcard 1932–1938*
- **Book 6:** *A Surface Creek Farewell 1939–1943*

To give the reader a sense of the *Champion*, I have included on the following page, a reduced image of the December 23, 1904 front page of the vintage newspaper. This sample is, of course, much smaller than the actual publication which was printed in a broadsheet format, making it somewhat larger than a modern newspaper. It is not intended to be readable, but is shown merely as an example. Digital versions of the *Champion* are, in most cases, crystal clear and can be substantially enlarged to facilitate readability.

SURFACE CREEK CHAMPION.

VOL. 1.   CEDAREDGE, COLORADO, DECEMBER 23, 1904.   NO. 24.

Great Excitement

Prevails in Delta over the Great Cut in Prices of DISHES. For two weeks we will sell These Goods at Exactly

Half Price

You Can't afford to miss this Chance of a Lifetime. We Also have an Excellent line of **Fancy China, Cut Glass etc. for Christmas Presents.** Come, See and be Convinced that this is the Greatest Bargain Ever Offered in These Goods.

F. P. Hunt & Co.

Delta, Colorado.

TIME GROWING SHORT.

The Last Week of the Contest will be a Busy one for Both this Office and the Contestants.

The contest closes on December 31st at 6 pm.

The subscription books will at all times during business hours be open to the inspection of candidates to enable them to obtain information upon which to work for votes.

No coupons will be sold from this office and none can be obtained by other means than as above set forth.

How to Get Votes.

This paper contains a coupon that may be clipped and voted, and each issue hereafter will contain such a coupon during the entire time of the contest.

Every subscriber paying upon subscription either back dues or in advance will receive coupons in the ratio of 100 votes for each $1 paid.

New subscriptions will also receive votes the same as those who pay up.

Subscriptions may be obtained anywhere, but the CHAMPION proposes to limit its candidates to ladies living contiguous to the publication.

Job work will be credited with votes in the ratio of one vote for every five cents paid for work.

For the present the ballot box will be located in the CHAMPION office.

The votes will be counted each Thursday by a committee composed of E. F. Graham, W. R.

Surface Creek Champion Ballot.	
Miss Essie Gipe	2040
Miss Ethel J. Steele	1415
Mrs. Grace Helland	519
Miss Myrtle Wood	601
Mrs. Lettie Doughty	100
Miss Winnie Dale	204
Miss Essie Jacques	1
Miss Josie Zanola	1

Jewelry at Cost.

From now until February 1st, 1904, I will offer my Entire line of Watches, Clocks, Jewelry, Cut Glass, Silver Ware, etc. at COST, for Cash Only. This does not mean 10 per cent. above cost, but Strictly

Manufacturing Cost

J. E. Clemings,

Delta's Leading Jeweler and Optician.

Surface Creek Champion Ballot.

This Ballot is good for ONE Vote in the

Gold Watch Contest

Cast for

The Supper.

The supper given by the ladies auxiliar in the Cedaredge hall last Thursday evening was a brilliant success both financially and socially. The two booths were handsomely decorated, one was presided over by the Busy Bees who sold dolls, toys and homemade candy. This booth netted about $14. The other booth was in charge of Mrs. Otis Hogrefe and contained a large quantity of useful and beautiful articles for the Christmas trade. The proceeds of this booth was a little over $90. The principal attraction of the evening was the supper and none that partook of this sumptuous repast had cause for complaint as everything was plentiful and well served. $54 was taken in from the supper.

About $20 worth of articles are still in the hands of Mrs. Hogrefe for sale.

The ladies who worked so faithfully for the successful outcome of this affair are certainly entitled to the thanks and congratulations of the community.

The members of this society expect to hold a supper and sale each year and have decided on next Thanksgiving as the date for next year.

Old papers for sale at this office.

SOUND + SENSE GIVING

There is both good will and good sense in giving gifts that combine Usefulness with Beauty. Our stock abounds in these sensible gifts.

Brushes	Hair, Clothe, Hat and Other Brushes, a little Finer than the regular kind. Prices low for the kind.
Toilet Sets	In a variety of Combinations. Can suit you on this Item.
Perfume	The kind that is always acceptable, Fancy packages and in bulk.
Leather Goods	Pocket Books and Purses for both Ladies and Gentlemen, Card Cases, Bill Books, etc
Stationery	Fine box Paper in Christmas boxes, Gold Pens, Letter Openers, Ink Wells, etc.

Yours for Business

The Seaton Drug Co.

Delta, Colorado.

The Play.

The Cory Dramatic club consisting of fourteen members, accompanied by a number of the young folks of that district, arrived in Cedaredge last Friday evening and presented the four act play entitled "Dot, the Miner's Daughter" to a large and appreciative audience in the hall. The club is under the management of Sam Ritter, and the play concluded with an excellent moral.

The parts were all well committed and rendered. After the conclusion of the play the crowd indulged in a social dance until midnight.

The Cory young people are a jolly crowd and we hope to see them visit this section again in the near future.

House Warming.

About 25 couples gathered at the new building, which has been erected by Wm. Hart for a pool room and barber shop. Monday evening and tripped the light fantastic until the small hours of the morning. The music was furnished by the Peterson orchestra, and an excellent oyster supper was served at midnight by J. B. Helland in the new hotel.

The evening passed all too quickly as everyone present report a very pleasant evening.

Lecture Course.

Wm. C. Millican will lecture on Japan and the recent acquisitions of the United States, at the Cedaredge hall next Tuesday and Thursday evenings. An admission of 15 and 25 cents will be charged and the proceeds will go to the Epworth League of the M. E. church. This lecture is the first of a course six or seven that the league is now trying to get. Mr. Millican is very highly spoken of as a lecturer and promises to give the people of this section an intellectual treat, so be sure and attend.

Delta.

From the Laborer.

In the county court Tuesday a divorce was granted to Mrs. Margurite A. Holmes from David A. Holmes on the grounds of extreme and repeated acts of cruelty.

The preliminary hearing of Joe Obergfell, charged with assault with intent to kill, was held before justice S. L. Fairlamb Saturday evening and the lad was bound over to the district court in the sum of $1000. The case will be taken before the district court on a writ of habeas corpus asking that the boy be tried in the juvenile court under the session laws of 1903.

At the delinquent tax sale of

Paonia.

From the Newspaper.

Early this week a half dozen of our enterprising citizens took up the matter of organizing a joint stock company to build a modern hotel. The structure they contemplate erecting will cost $10,000 according to their estimates.

The rumor that Mr. Bruce would make a public hall out of the building now occupied by Reynolds & Dix has become a fact. Mr. Bruce will take out the partition and refloor the building and perhaps put in a stage. He will also build upon the lot just north of his store and expects to run a wholesale and retail ice cream store.

From the Gazette.

Somerset broke all former records last Thursday when it mined and shipped 925 tons, or 48 cars of coal. The increasing output of this camp will prove one of the factors in securing a broad gauge for this branch, which the writer confidently expects will be put in next spring.

Sam Lovett thinks that there are some parties in Cedaredge who were weaned too soon. He left a small pail of fresh milk at the store Monday evening while he went to the dance a short time, during his absence someone drank the milk and replaced it with water. And the worst of it is that Sam carried the bucket carefully home as usual and did not know the difference until the next morning when he had to face his coffee straight.

Delta county a record breaking sale was made which goes a long way to prove that this is the most prosperous county in Colorado and capital is eager to invest here. Less than $200 was the amount of property that the county was compelled to buy in for taxes and that was for improvements on public lands.

At the last term of the district court an injunction was issued against R. Dove restraining him from in any way interfering with certain ditches in his neighborhood. It seems that he has not paid much attention to the order of the court and has been cutting ditches at pleasure and Judge Stevens demanded his presence before him Thursday to show cause why he should not be punished for contempt of court. In some way the peaceful Dove has acquired a reputation as being a very bad man, defying officers and law, so Deputy Sheriffs French and Rhoades went after him Wednesday and brought him in to Delta and Sheriff Hunt conveyed him to Ouray to see the judge.

The attendance at the Cedaredge school during the first part of the term has been excellent, only out of an enrollment of 80 only five have dropped out. It is expected that there will be several new scholars after the holidays

---

Doings at Cory.

Special Correspondence.

(Too late for last week.)

Lee Snelson returned from Denver last Friday.

Mrs. S. Phoenix has been quite sick for several days.

Rev. Knight preached at the Fairview school house last Sunday.

Mr. Gifford and wife of Silverton are visiting their daughter, Mrs. W. R. Lyle.

Chas. Darlington was down from Hotchkiss for a few days visiting his mother, Mrs. John Lyons.

The literary society at the Mound school house is a great success, come out and enjoy yourself every Thursday evening.

Jim Manges and "Happy Hooligan" returned Saturday from an outing and hunting trip on the San Miguel river loaded down with game, nit.

Smethurst and Thore Thompson and the result announced each week in this paper.

❧ Introduction ❧

Writing in 1977, the late journalist and author Hazel Baker Austin opened the second edition of her *Surface Creek Country* with an explanatory note which neatly forms an introduction to the present volume. Some of the contents of her book, reported as fact by those she interviewed, need to be taken with a grain of salt. However, her work is a good starting point for anyone interested in Surface Creek history. Her brief explanation of the Surface Creek Valley is wonderfully concise and descriptive:

> *"The term Surface Creek Country came into general use by early settlers to designate the valley that comprised the lowlands watered by Surface Creek, Tongue Creek, Ward Creek, Dry Creek and their tributaries. The area of this valley is about 14 miles long and varies from three to eight miles in width and covers the territory from Grand Mesa on the north to the Gunnison River on the south."* —Hazel Baker Austin

The United States Forest Service considers the region to be the Surface Creek Drainage. Those who call this beautiful spot home have adopted a more lyrical phrase. We call it the Surface Creek Valley.

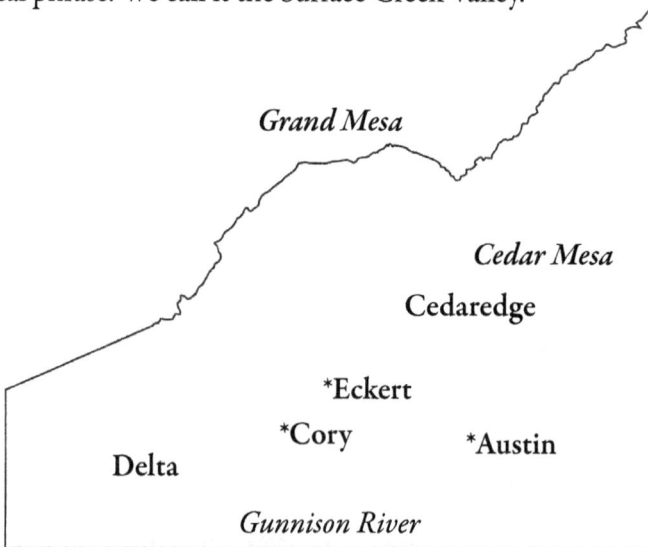

Grand Mesa

Cedar Mesa

Cedaredge

*Eckert

*Cory   *Austin

Delta

Gunnison River

Communities in the Surface Creek Valley
of Delta County, Colorado
Part of the statutory town of Orchard City

Christmas 1904

The *Surface Creek Champion* is a mere five months old as the newspaper celebrates its first Christmas. The mercury manages to climb to 37 degrees after an icy overnight low of 27. Nearly three inches of fresh snow fall in Grand Junction and brief flurries descend on Cedaredge, but a Christmas Day storm leaves only a trace of moisture in the Surface Creek Valley.

Though temperatures are quite chilly, the *Champion's* ambitious "Gold Watch Contest" provides plenty of heat and not a few fireworks. Conceived by the fledgling newspaper to boost subscriptions, the contest offers a gold watch to whichever Surface Creek female can garner the most votes.

> **Surface Creek Champion Ballot.**
>
> This Ballot is good for ONE Vote in the
>
> **Gold   Watch   Contest**
>
> Cast for
>
> M _____

The contest is essentially a popularity competition which invites voters to use whatever criteria they wish to select their favorite Surface Creek female. The prized gold watch itself is on display at the Cedaredge general store operated by Meyer & Doughty. According to the *Champion's* report: "Every-body says (the watch) is a beauty and several ladies who have seen it went to work immediately rustling new subscribers. Now," the newspaper declared, "is the time to hustle for your favorite."

Knocking the concept of one-person-one-vote on its ear, balloting in the gold watch competition can be enhanced up to one-hundred-fold by a voter who renews or begins a *Champion* subscription. Anyone who purchases job printing from the newspaper can likewise enhance their votes.

Author's note: Lest the reader think that the Champion *was alone in launching such a contest, holding competitions to boost new subscriptions was a common practice among newspapers large and small. And rewarding those who renewed subscriptions, paid overdue bills, or purchased printing services by allowing those parties to enhance their votes was also widely accepted.*

The gold watch contest had begun in early November 1904 with voting scheduled to continue apace until the close of December. Christmas-time totals place Miss Essie Gipe first among eight nominated contestants. A popular young woman, Miss Gipe is noted for her reading at the Methodist Episcopal Easter celebration and for her work with the town's Elberta Rebekah Lodge where she serves as recording secretary.

Author's note: Only a month earlier, Miss Gipe—who was apparently a charmer—was voted "handsomest lady present" by the Cedaredge Chapter of Woodmen of the World at their November entertainment and basket social. To commemorate this earlier honor, Miss Gipe received "a fine gold chain." At the self-same Woodmen's event, Dr. I.F. Burgin was voted homeliest gentleman present, for which he good-naturedly accepted the gift of a looking glass.

Returning to the November–December 1904 Gold Watch Contest, as of Christmas Day Miss Essie Gipe leads all-comers with 2,040 votes. In second place, with 1,413 votes, is Miss Ethel J. Steele. Also nominated, but well off the pace are (in descending order of votes tallied): Mrs. Grace Helland, Miss Myrtle Wood, Mrs. Lettie Doughty, Miss Winnie Dale, Miss Essie Jacques, and Miss Josie Zanola—although the last two young ladies have only a single vote apiece.

Alas, Miss Gipe's seemingly insurmountable lead dwindles in the closing days of the contest when a last-minute avalanche of votes for Mrs. Grace Helland puts her in the lead with an astounding total of 7,092 votes, besting Miss Gipe's final tally of 6,046. Mrs. Helland's victory is a popular choice for the well-known woman who serves as the town's milliner, keeping local women supplied with the latest in fashionable lady's hats. Later, in the coming year,

Mrs. Helland would achieve an additional measure of celebrity for her performance in the Cedaredge Hall production of "Ten Nights in a Bar Room."

Author's note: The play "Ten Nights in a Bar Room" is based on an 1854 novel entitled "Ten Nights in a Bar Room and What I Saw There," by Timothy Shay Arthur, an American author. Generally speaking, the play was intended to promote prohibition. During the 1850s, Arthur's book was so popular that only Harriet Beecher Stowe's "Uncle Tom's Cabin" exceeded its sales. The local productions in the Surface Creek Valley were undoubtedly enhanced by the fact that the action takes place in the fictional town of "Cedarville." Whether the subject matter was performed as serious theatre or as a tongue-in-cheek satire, is anybody's guess. But, given the times and the stature of persons acting the parts, it seems likely that it was presented as a cautionary tale with a not too subtle moral.

In other theatrical news, the Cory Dramatic Club arrives in Cedaredge to present a four-act morality play entitled "Dot, the Miner's Daughter." A large and appreciative audience gathers in Cedaredge Hall for the performance. Sam Ritter, who manages the dramatic club, brings along a number of young folks from the Cory area and it is reported that the Cory youngsters are "a jolly crowd" and Cedaredge hopes the youths will return in the near future.

School news is encouraging. Attendance at the Cedaredge School has been "exceedingly good" with only five dropping out of an enrollment of 99. Several new scholars are expected to enroll after the holidays. Miss Smith, a new teacher, has been installed in the Trickle School which is situated several miles below Cedaredge.

Author's note: The names Trickle and Trickel appear often in the pages of the Champion. *Although the news stories are not always consistent, it seems that Trickel refers to a Grand Mesa reservoir by that name and possibly to a bridge which apparently spanned Surface Creek in the Eckert vicinity. The bridge is said to have marked the general boundary between the upper and lower Surface Creek Valley and may even have been used as a dividing line between voting precincts. Trickle seems to refer to the school and at least one extended family. However, Trickel sometimes appears as a family name. For purposes of this book, and the author's sanity, the names will have to be considered interchangeable.*

At Pannell School, boys and girls have thrown themselves into the work of planning an entertainment—enthusiasm which leads to success and gladdens a teacher's heart. According to the school's special correspondent: "The days pass pleasantly when preparing the Christmas decorations and much amusement has been derived from extra cotton batting left over from the (holiday) letters. It makes excellent mustaches and whiskers for some of the boys."

Cedaredge night life gets a boost when fifty people brave chilly temperatures to attend a house warming at a new building erected by Wm. Hart. The building will house the apparently compatible activities of pool room and barber shop. Couples dance to the music of the Peterson orchestra and enjoy an excellent oyster supper served at midnight by J.B. Helland in the town's new hotel. Hart's advertisement adds soft drinks, confectionery, and cigars to his list of goods and invites customers to stop by "for a smooth shave or a quiet game of pool."

Author's note: Based on advertisements announcing proprietors and amenities, ownership of Cedaredge's pool and billiard halls, with or without a connected bowling alley, periodically changed hands. A 1904 Champion *article suggested that Wm. Hart built the first structure intended to house a pool room as well as a barber shop and cigar emporium. The multiple uses may have been compatible since someone waiting for a shave or haircut could have a smoke and pass the time at a pool table. In 1905, Hart reportedly added another pool table. Sometime between December 1905 and 1906, W.A. Tim set up the Cedaredge*

Confectionary featuring pool, a bowling alley, and holiday candy and nuts. Whether Tim inherited Hart's operation is unclear. By 1909, J.L. Patterson is announced as proprietor of the Cedaredge Billiard Hall with connected bowling alley. In 1910, Eckert opened its own barber shop/pool hall consortium. As for the location of the Cedaredge facility, an unconfirmed rumor is that it was once located in the building which, until recently, housed the Short Branch Liquor Store at 130 North Grand Mesa Drive/Highway 65. A 1915 fire insurance map shows a building at that general location with a long narrow construct extending west from the rear of a small rectangular building—and looking suspiciously like a one-lane bowling alley. If this was indeed the site of one of the town's early recreation centers, that wooden, forest green structure was torn down to make way for the PUR CannaBliss cannabis dispensary which opened in 2022.

In regional news, the town of Somerset shatters all previous records when its latest mining and shipping-yield tops 925 tons—a harvest of coal which fills 43 railcars. A sturdy locomotive traction engine, designed to haul coal from the Fairview mine, has taken up its station at the Cory switch. A committee of Paonia citizens have organized a joint stock company with an eye toward raising $10,000 to build a modern hotel.

In anticipation of holiday visitors, A.E. Miller, who serves as proprietor of the Cedaredge Hotel and Lodging House is advertising "clean and comfortable beds and table supplied with all that the season affords" adding that the "regular stage to Delta arrives and departs from the hotel" and that the hotel boasts an attached livery and feed stable.

Not to be outdone, Miller's kin, who operates the Cedaredge Hack Line, reminds readers that his horse-drawn conveyance "carries the mails and passengers (from) Delta to Cedaredge and intermediate points" as well as delivering parcels. The younger Miller's motto: "Comfortable Vehicles, Speedy Teams, Good Roads."

In addition to displaying the gold watch to be awarded in the year-end newspaper contest, Meyer & Doughty welcome the winter season with "a large stock of comforts and bed blankets at very low prices." The proprietors also remind potential suppliers that their New Store pays the highest market price for butter, eggs, poultry, and hides. E.F. Graham, Cedaredge's black-smith and wagon maker, announces that he specializes in horse shoeing and tire setting.

Surface Creek merchants are hoping for a pros-perous holiday season. Reynolds & King Brothers of Eckert are promoting their establishment as "sole agents in the Surface Creek Valley for the Hamilton Brown Shoe Company's famous boots and shoes." A timely claim, since the Brown Shoe Company has just acquired the name and character rights to the Buster Brown comic strip character and the combination has become an instant hit with consumers.

Clubs and churches announce their holiday meetings. The literary soci-ety of Mound School House meets every Thursday. The Methodist Episco-pal Church will erect a Christmas tree for children on Christmas night and hold a special New Year service on the evening of January 1. The Peach Belt Lodge, International Order of Odd Fellows, meet on Wednesday evening. Woodmen of the World, Cedaredge Camp, meets Saturdays and Women of Woodcraft, Cedaredge Circle, meet on Tuesdays. Two unions of the Order of Washington meet on alternate Saturdays and will sponsor a dance at the Cedaredge Hall on the evening of December 30. The usual admission of $1.25 will be charged.

Author's note: Cedaredge Hall, which is often mentioned as the site of meetings and entertainments, was constructed in 1903 by a group of local citizens who recognized the need for a general meeting place. The hall was the first building erected on the western edge of town and one of the few with two stories. For many years the lower floor housed commercial enterprises. The Meyer and Doughty general merchandise store was the first occupant. The roomy upstairs of the hall became the center for community activities until 1920, when a school auditorium was built. Plays, socials, dinners, dances, church services, the first mov-ing picture shows, and regular lodge meetings took place in the well-used facility. The place was so popular that it was often difficult for local interests to schedule an open night. Over the years, the hall fell into disuse and the Cedaredge landmark was torn down in 1940.

Several items of social and community interest provide a glimpse into local life. On a sad note, Miss Effie Harris, aged 30 years, daughter of Mr. and Mrs. J.S. Harris, has passed away. A Gipe family reunion takes place on Christmas Day. The gathering is a gala event which welcomes 60 family members. Word comes that G.H. Webb and the Surface Creek Grower's Association received silver medals for apples exhibited at the recent St. Louis Fair. H.A. Stolte received a bronze medal. Parker Hart is reported to have shot an owl which measures 54 inches from the tip of one wing to the tip of the other. Just in time for Christmas, Mr. and Mrs. John Hawkins are the happy parents of a fine baby girl.

Visiting orator, Wm. C. Millican, lectures on Japan and recent acquisitions of the United States, including the Philippines. Admission is set at 15 cents for children and 25 cents for adults, with proceeds going to the Epworth League of the Methodist Episcopal Church. The talk draws only a small crowd, but organizers plan a second lecture and hope for a better turnout when the weather improves.

The Cedaredge Ladies Auxiliary—affiliated with the local Baptist congregation—nets nearly $150 selling Christmas trade items and serving a sumptuous supper. Prior to the holiday sale, nineteen ladies of the Auxiliary braved a brief snowstorm to sew goods. The sale includes candy and nuts, a sofa pillow booth, a doll booth, and a *Ladies Home Journal* booth featuring donated goods and opportunities to subscribe to the *Journal*. A table of handsome chinaware is also on display. The Auxiliary supper features roast turkey, baked chicken, scalloped oysters and all the trimmings. Next year, booth displays will be erected and supper will be served during milder weather and closer to Thanksgiving.

Miss Anna Perry has relocated to Delta to study music. She will be gone all winter. A.H. Stockham has purchased a 30-foot lot on the new town site. As an early Christmas present to the growing town, he is contemplating erecting a good bank building there in the near future.

Just after Christmas, and before the New Year commences, Mr. G.O. Anderson and Miss Pearl Coquelette will be married. The bride is the daughter of Mrs. Davis who lives on Third Street. The groom is presently mining in Ouray and was previously employed by the Denver & Rio Grande Railroad for which he helped in the construction of flumes to convey needed water.

Harry Lingren, who attends the state agricultural college at Fort Collins, is home for the holidays. F.W. Childs offers a good milk cow for sale. A.A. Weir has scheduled a post-Christmas auction sale at his ranch near Eckert. Ollie Buzzard is "very low with pneumonia fever," but—at last report—is some better. W.E. Hurley is selling the following, cheap: one good work mare, two colts, one spring wagon, one cow, 100 white leghorn hens, and one incubator.

Author's note: The reader will notice that the opening years of this narrative are relatively brief, whereas the summaries of later years grow longer. Initially, local news in the Champion *was sparse compared to the space devoted to "canned" features and advertisements. Occasionally, the editor would publish brief articles imploring readers to send him news. As Clyde W. Brewer gained experience with his community and confidence in his craft, and when designated correspondents began to generate news, the ratio of articles to ads and features achieved balance. Eventually, when Brewer was hitting his stride as a local journalist, rumor has it that he experimented with dropping the canned content only to reinstate it when readers rebelled. As it happens, the reading public enjoyed the patent medicine advertisements, features about fashions and culture, tidbits of world and national news, special items for children, cartoons and jokes, and especially the serialized fictions.*

Christmas 1905

Just before Christmas break, thirty-six Cedaredge School pupils are recognized for being neither absent nor tardy for the month of November. Cited for perfect and timely attendance are Glen Atchison; Joe and Hartzel Benefiel; Minnie Childs; Percy Garton; Cecyl, Iona and Frances Dolph; Edith, Fred and Frank Maxwell; Guilford and Alva Gipe; Lyle Lambert; Guy and Bessie Pickett; Rose and Lettia Motto; Jessie and Neva Skinner; Opal Sisk; Mary and Anna Zaninetti; Dana, Delia, Fern, and Venus Reeves; Edwin and Lester Riley; Frankie Griffith; Ruby Hart; Nora McGruder; Mabel Woodward; Greta Van Aken; Della Giddings; and Henry Rhoads. In other Cedaredge School news, a window pane was accidentally broken by a boy in the lower grades and his playmates generously helped make up the money to replace it.

Cedaredge School is becoming so crowded that it will soon be necessary to add another room to the present building or rent a room elsewhere. Another teacher will also be needed. If the rate of growth continues, it may be necessary to build another school house and possibly add a high school to avoid the necessity for children to go to Delta or elsewhere after completing the eighth grade. As of this winter, the enrollment in the Cedaredge School is 122 pupils.

The Surface Creek Valley gets a white Christmas with two inches of snow and the day is cold with a high of 35 and an overnight low which some folks say reached four degrees. The official record was ten degrees, but it probably felt colder. The snow and cold temperatures came as a shock to the Valley which had been experiencing, throughout December 1905, splendid weather with days so pleasant it hardly seemed like winter.

Optimistic talk in Cory concerns an electric line being strung in the vicinity. Miss Mignon Kennicott has been elected president of the literary society. Work has begun on the Dry Creek Ditch, but on account of it being frozen, labor has been stopped until warmer weather. Christmas trees will be on display at both the Mound and Fairview school houses.

Eckert is sponsoring a turkey raffle with the prize to be awarded on December 23. Skating is reported to be good on the basin reservoir. Chas. W. McMurray is ill with typhoid pneumonia. Eckert resident Elias Wenger has plans to break a team of mules before Christmas. His neighbors advise: "If you see anything coming so fast you can't see it, that's Wenger and the mules."

Miss Effie Gipe will be greatly missed as she and other relations have re-located to Los Angeles.

Cedaredge and Surface Creek residents are continuing to discuss the wisdom of establishing a Board of Trade or other organization whose purpose is to enhance economic development of the region. A series of pre-holiday meetings have been well attended and a subcommittee of citizens have recommended the establishment of a permanent organization under the name of The Surface Creek Improvement Association of Cedaredge. The purpose of the association shall be "the promotion of the general welfare of the Surface Creek country."

Cedar Mesa citizens are canvassing the community for donations of work or money to construct a new road. The goal is to "make an easier grade to the mesa, as the old grade is very steep in some places and a load of produce or provisions cannot be hauled up without a great deal of exertion on the part of the (horse) team." The newly proposed road, while longer, will only have about a six-percent grade. Work will commence in December with a force of 10–15 men engaged and continue depending on weather. It is hoped the new road will be completed in time for Christmas. A road leading west from Cedaredge is also being completed and will soon be ready for travel.

The F.P. Hunt & Company enterprise of Delta is offering to roast anyone's holiday turkey in their large, roomy, and ventilated oven. Takers won't need to baste their turkey because Buck's Roomy Oven is a self-basting appliance.

Surface Creek residents John A. McKinnon and Myra Trickle were wed at the Odd Fellows' Hall in Delta. They will make their home at the lower end of Cedar Mesa. Hugh Galligher, a popular passenger conductor on the Denver & Rio Grande Railroad, has been all over the country, but—having seen it all—has decided to put down stakes in the Surface Creek Valley.

A reprise of the memorable play "Ten Nights in a Bar Room" will take place just before Christmas. The popular entertainment will include the tableau "Little Mary, an Angel in Heaven." Theatre goers are advised to watch for big posters advertising the event. Wm. Hart's new bowling alley has been completed and opened for business in time for the holidays. Hart has also added another pool table. Wm. Skinner has leased the McGruder coal mine on Cedar Mesa and will begin taking out what he hopes will be a good grade of coal.

The Presbyterian Ladies' Aid Society of Eckert will hold a pre-holiday bazaar and New England supper at Eckert Hall. A fine umbrella was found abandoned on the Surface Creek Road between Cory and Eckert. The owner can reclaim same by seeing Harry Ferguson, providing they can prove ownership of the property and are willing to pay the cost of the published lost and found notice.

Merchants are gearing up for Christmas. Blanchard & Stockham invite the public to "come in and see our Christmas dolls and toys"—a full line on hand at right prices. The Seaton Drug Company, with outlets in Cedaredge and Delta, offers candy, candles, fine perfumes, books, stationary, and toiletries—all gifts handsomely boxed. Wm. W. Hart's Cedaredge store features

Christmas candies, nuts and sweet meats, as well as a full line of cigars and tobacco—promising that the latter includes "any kind on Earth."

James Zaninetti offers Cedaredge town lots averaging from $40 to $200, according to location. Also for sale are 800 acres of land adjoining the town which will be sold "in small tracts at reasonable prices and easy terms." Chas. D. Gutshall, manager of the Cory Lumber & Mercantile Company invites shoppers to "save the long haul from Delta" by purchasing locally available lumber, building materials, hardware, wire, and groceries. Mr. Sanford of the Co-operative Telephone Company reports the system is having a very prosperous year.

In agricultural news, Frank Teachout of Eckert sold his crop of hay for a good figure. The price of hay continues to rise. Area farmers are counting up the profits for this year's sugar beet season. Of the 9,480 tons attributed to Delta County farmers, Cory accounts for 40 railroad cars, or roughly 800 tons. The nearly 10,000 tons produced by Delta County growers is an increase over last year of over 6,800 tons. Surface Creek farmer J.A. Luellen received a second-place prize for pears exhibited at the Pueblo State Fair. He was so near to getting first that it took the judges several days to make a decision.

Austin will soon be home to a new finishing mill which will add the convenience of readily available planed lumber to the Surface Creek building community. Several Cory residents were ill but are improving. There is talk of an electric railway in the Cory area.

A new counterfeit ten-dollar bill is circulating. The bogus money may be recognized by its size, which is longer than the genuine note. A citizen suggests that what is wanted is a ten-dollar bill which will not only look longer, but last longer.

Christmas spirit was sadly lacking just days before the holiday. The Peterson Brothers, local musicians, made arrangements for a big pre-Christmas dance to be staged at the Cedaredge Hall. Unfortunately, the evening turned ugly when men who over-indulged on whiskey created a disturbance. Two men had a disagreement over an alleged theft and a third man, who attempted to settle the argument, was stabbed in the chest. Happily, the wound was not fatal, but the assailant was badly beaten by others before he could be arrested and jailed.

Frank W. Childs has fruit land for sale. A jack-of-all-trades, Mr. Childs also offers fire insurance, loans, and notary public services.

The Delta firm of Geer & Clack have holiday offerings of new furniture, carpets, linoleum, curtain poles, shades, curtains, and picture frames. And the enterprising businessmen are also willing to serve as funeral directors and licensed embalmers.

Christmas 1906

Shall we incorporate? As the holidays approach, the *Surface Creek Champion* newspaper exhorts readers to consider the benefits of incorporating the growing settlement of Cedaredge into a proper town. The *Champion* feels a majority of citizens favor such a move and advocates that an incorporation vote be taken this winter. The first step is to convince 30 property owners to sign a petition which will be sent to a Delta County judge. Upon receipt of a valid petition, a judge has the authority to issue an order of election and, if voters are in favor of incorporation, that same judge can issue an additional order for the election of town officers.

An issue which causes some locals to resist incorporation is the question of boundaries. One proposal is to take in approximately one square mile, with the cornerstone near the present post office serving as center. It is understood that a corporation may take into its limits any piece of land which is less than 40 acres and do so without the consent of the owner. Tracts of 40 acres or more require the owner's consent to place such land in the incorporated town limits.

In 1906, newspaper publisher Clyde W. Brewer had a vision of an incorporated town. Cedaredge was ultimately established in 1907.

At present, there are three or four 40-acre tracts within the proposed incorporation square which will have to be left out as the owners do not care to come in. But the remainder of the anticipated townsite needs only a majority consent of voters living within the proposed limits.

Some argue that Cedaredge is, at present, too small to incorporate and that the expenses associated with this move will be too great. The *Champion* estimates incorporation would cost about $150, an expense which would be shared by property owners within the proposed town limits—the share of each owner being based upon the value of a given property. Size and improvements are measures of property value and owners of larger and improved property, the *Champion* maintains, will be able to stand the expense.

The holdings of all property owners—both land and buildings—will, the *Champion* believes, be enhanced by incorporation. According to the newspaper, the act of incorporation will protect property holders from threats "which, if carried out, would result in giving the place one of the worst names a town can get. When a lot of roughs get to running a town, it is time something was done."

Author's note: The threats to Cedaredge's future reputation are not named, but the implication seems to be that an unincorporated area runs the risk of having undesirable outcomes in the form of disorganized growth, not to mention gambling, liquor, prostitution, and crime.

The newspaper also believes that, without an organized body to handle things, needed improvements will not be made. Writing in favor of incorporation, Clyde W. Brewer makes an impassioned, front-page appeal:

"We need sidewalks," Brewer declares, "and streets graded, now, and will later want waterworks, light plant and other things of this nature, and we believe the town should own these itself and not let it get into the hands of some corporation that will make a big thing out of it with little return to the town. These things are apt to come about at any time and want an organized body to handle them properly. It is always the best plan to prepare ahead as no one knows what will come up that needs immediate attention."

Within days of this call to action, a petition is being circulated and sufficient signatures are collected to insure an election. An informal census of people residing in the incorporation area suggests that as many as 200 are present within the proposed limits.

"Bud" McMurray, an Eckert resident and member of that settlement's McMurray Ranch crowd, sketched a December 1906 front page cartoon in honor of a colorful local character who operates the Cedaredge to Delta stage coach. W.T. "Dad" Lambert's rig is one of a handful of horse-drawn "hacks" which move mail, cargo, and people up and down the Surface Creek Valley.

"DAD" LAMBERT AND HIS STAGE ON THE ROAD TO DELTA.
Drawn for the Champion by "Bud" McMurray of Eckert.

The weather has been stormy and disagreeable with snow and rain falling much of the time. The condition of the roads point to the need for sidewalks. The moisture, however, is making the farmer very happy.

After five years in business, Joseph Hogrefe, who is remembered as the first active merchant in Cedaredge, sold his merchandise to J.L. Shurd. Originally from Steamboat Springs, Shurd will continue the business and promises to carry a more complete line of goods. Shurd will retain the community service of an active post office and he plans to work as teller in the newly proposed bank building.

Returns from sales of this year's peach harvest show promise for this crop. Eckert residents W.E. Steele and Arthur King report record earnings. In other orchard news, G.H. Webb has received notice from Denver that the state board of horticulture and the national grange committee have awarded prizes for his display of nine different varieties of apples. Western slope exhibitors swept the competition with Montezuma County placing first, Montrose second, Delta third, and Mesa fourth.

Mr. Hotchkiss of Colona is in Cedaredge with his threshing outfit which is bound for the Dry Creek section. Half a mile east of town is a very bad strip of road which has been made worse by recent storms. When one of the lead traction engines reached the bad road, it got stuck fast in the mud. With much effort, the machinery was extracted and crews set to work on W.S. Gorsuch's large crop of grain.

The furnace which heats the Eckert School continues to be a problem. To remedy the situation, the school board is placing stoves in schoolrooms much to the delight of pupils and teachers. The upper rooms and more mature students who attend there plan an extensive program for Christmas. This holiday program follows on the heels of a well-received Thanksgiving program presented by the younger students. Teachers Miss Potts and Mrs. Hopson are commended for their work on the Thanksgiving program.

Cedaredge School enrolls new students Lulu Gipe, Henry Rhoads, Edward Webb, and Clarence Griffith. The enrollment now includes 37 pupils in Mr. Benefiel's charge; 40 in Miss Zeigler's room; and 50 students with Mrs. Benefiel.

At the Pannell School, Miss Cunningham holds a pleasing afternoon session for the benefit of the children's parents. The schoolhouse is shining with the results of applying soap and water and installing fresh curtains. Surrounded by Christmas decorations, nearly every child of the 27 enrolled spoke his or her Christmas piece. Then all received a Christmas treat. Mr. George Morris is teaching at Pannell during the absence of Miss Peare who has been called away to Kansas City to settle her late father's estate. As matters there will keep her occupied for some time, she has reluctantly resigned her position here.

In Eckert, Mr. and Mrs. Bert Campbell are the proud parents of twin babies. In Tongue Creek, six boys enrolled in the 8th grade are surprised with a test in grammar which they mastered and enjoyed.

J.J. January receives word of the death of his brother in South Dakota. The late brother had served as a Union soldier in the Civil War. Captured and imprisoned in a southern stockade, he had endured hardships including having to amputate both feet using only his pocket knife.

Appealing to holiday shoppers, J.W. Edmons, a Delta-based jeweler announces a "Great Slaughter Sale" of an overstock of watches, clocks, silverware, hand-painted china, and sundry jewelry. Ramsay Dry Goods of Delta, which company bills itself as "Santa Claus's Home," is also advertising a gigantic holiday sale and they warn that "Late-comers get Poor Picking."

A movement is afoot to rename Dirty George Creek. Proponents of the change lament "the idea of calling one of the prettiest, purest, cleanest little stream of water in the state by such a name. It is an insult to clean water and the stream referred to is certainly entitled to a more respectable title."

Cedaredge's own firm of Buzzard & Sons is offering fresh meats.

The Colorado Telephone Company, one of two providers seeking subscribers, is advertising low

Fresh Meats

Of all kinds constantly on hand. You needn't be afraid of getting tainted meat from us as we have one of the finest refrigerators in the county. You will also receive the most courteous treatment. We also carry a full line of

Salt and Smoked Meats

Shop Open from 7 a. m. to 8 p. m.

Buzzard & Sons.

rates and a promise to help users keep in touch with their children who might be in the city attending school. Their service, they maintain, will keep community members "in close touch with the world. Just as easy to talk with children in the city hundreds of miles away as to talk to your neighbor half a mile down the road."

Another story on the Colorado Telephone Company announces a reduction in the rate to rent an instrument. Still, this rate reduction leaves them costing more than the local homegrown Delta County Co-operative Telephone Exchange.

A mountain lion is sighted north of Cedaredge. A local resident attempts to make a name for himself by killing the beast only to discover that he's mistakenly shot a horse blanket which had been stretched over a chair.

The ranch known as the Butt & Finch Place encompasses 120 acres northwest of Cedaredge. It is rumored to have sold for $13,000.

A representative of a Nebraska real estate firm brought more than a dozen prospective settlers to Delta County. A few made their way to Cedar Mesa where C.B. Pickett instantly purchased 40 acres with the intention of returning soon to reside there. Other potential settlers purchased several town lots.

Cedaredge is temporarily without an operating hotel. After the present hotel closed, a party from Kentucky was to arrive to take charge, but—after looking things over—the man and wife decided the place was not for them. For weeks, while the status of the hotel hung in the balance, the lack of a hotel discouraged visitors. To the rescue comes J.H. Dale who pledges to take charge of the hotel immediately and operate it as a first-class establishment.

Word comes that the River Portal of Gunnison Tunnel has passed the first mile of its "great bore." This welcome news is eclipsed by an errant drill which strikes a tremendous flow of water accompanied by a dangerous volume of flammable gas. Work is temporarily halted.

The Cedaredge firm of Lovett's Livery, Feed and Sale Stable offers fine rigs and good, safe teams.

Twenty visitors from the Delta Odd Fellows Lodge are treated to a fine oyster supper at the Cedaredge Lodge. The Cedaredge gun club plans a New Year's Eve dance.

W.E. Pullen and wife have moved into their newly acquired ranch on Upper Tongue Creek. The house they vacated in town has been occupied by W.S. Grant, town blacksmith. J.C. Rowbotham and family have plans to occupy their 40-acre spread north of Cedaredge as soon as their residence is completed. Otis Hogrefe and his wife are pleased with their Austin ranch where the soil is very deep and of good quality. Hogrefe and several other new arrivals are constructing a ditch to irrigate the land.

A big dance takes place at the Eckert Hall on Christmas night. Funds raised by the dance and accompanying supper will go toward purchasing more instruments for the fledgling band. Also at Eckert Hall, the Ladies Auxiliary of the Baptist Church hold a Christmas sale which includes entertainment and a box supper. Christmas entertainments are given at the Central and Trickle Schools. A band dance on Christmas night draws a large crowd who enjoy vocal selections by John Bowers. While playing baseball last week, Eckert resident Chas. Taft had the misfortune of getting his thumb broke.

Author's note: To conserve time, ink, and paper, first names in vintage documents were often abbreviated using a standard list of substitutes. Those researching family histories often encounter such abbreviations especially on census records and in passenger lists. Some, such as Chas. *for* Charles, *are somewhat obvious. Other recognizable examples are* Sar. *for* Sarah, Jas. *for* James, *and* Robt. *for* Robert. *Some are not so obvious, such as* Xpr. *for* Christopher *or* My. *for* Mary.

A letter from J.M. Woodward, State Game and Fish Commissioner informs the public that mountain sheep are perpetually protected. Colorado state legislation once allowed the killing of mountain sheep, but that law has been rescinded.

The Denver & Rio Grande Railroad announces annual holiday rates for Christmas and New Year's. Passengers traveling between December 22 and January 4 are eligible for reduced fares to all points in Colorado and New Mexico. The J.K. Grant building is nearly completed. When open for business, Mr. Grant will carry a line of groceries and livestock feed.

Author's note: Still standing at 260 West Main Street, the Grant building continues to serve local residents as a downtown Cedaredge coffeeshop and social gathering place.

A faithful *Champion* advertiser, the Seaton Drug Company touts holiday specials at its stores in Delta and Cedaredge. Bargains include a large assortment of Christmas candies—chocolates, creams, caramels, and figs. These treats range from 20 to 65 cents per pound. The store also carries perfumes in fancy boxes; books ranging from poetry to juvenile stories to novels; fancy stationary; Christmas cards; meerschaum pipes; pocketbooks; and cigars.

In one of many "Desert-Land, Final Proof" notices, the United States Land Office of Montrose, Colorado, acknowledges that Charles B. Pickett of Cedaredge, Colorado, has filed notice of intention to make proof on his desert-land claim number 756 Ute. A legal description follows, citing section, township, and range. Witnesses to prove that Pickett has performed "complete irrigation and reclamation of said land" are listed as John M. James, Robert P. James, Virgil Atchison, and Allen Hardman, all of Cedaredge.

Author's note: In the early 1900's, most issues of the Surface Creek Champion *newspaper included a steady stream of legal notices of an individual's intent to "make proof" on a "desert-land claim." Land claims carried the designation "Ute" and were uniquely numbered to specify a particular section, township, and range. Each intention was accompanied by witness testimony that the intended party had completed irrigation and reclamation activities. The land in question had once been the ancestral home of a western band of the Ute Tribe. The Ute's land was seized and opened for settlement in the wake of the Meeker Incident. In September 1879, Nathan Meeker was an Indian agent working on the White River Ute Reservation just west of present-day Meeker, Colorado. Fueled by disagreements, a group of Utes attacked the agency, killing Meeker and his male employees and taking women and children hostage. On that same day, Utes fought with a detachment of the U.S. Army at Milk Creek, just north of present-day Meeker. The detachment's commanding officer and a dozen troops were killed. Relief troops dispersed the Utes. Hostages were released, but hostility toward the Utes increased. After treaty negotiations failed to reach a resolution, the U.S. Congress stepped in. Repudiating earlier treaties, Congress passed The Ute Removal Act—legislation which led to the forced removal of Uncompahgre and White River Utes to Utah. Settlers, ranchers, miners, and farmers soon arrived and laid claim to the land through the final proof process.*

G.H. Webb has received a pair of shoes which he won at this fall's state fair. Delivered much after the fact, the shoes seem to have arrived as a result of publicity and agitation over their delay. A jury deliberating far into the night has found Leon Todd Smith not guilty of cattle stealing.

Mrs. E.L. Rhoades of Delta is going to open a bakery in Cedaredge as soon as a building can be prepared. She has her eye on a little structure next to Rock's blacksmith shop. Her specialty will be fresh-baked bread.

A pair of fighting dogs brought Mrs. W.H. Giddings to harm. The animals were fighting near her door. When she attempted to part them, one of the dogs turned on her and "chewed her right hand in a frightful manner. One of the small bones was torn entirely from the hand and it is feared that the entire member will have to be amputated. She is suffering a great deal of pain."

The Eckert firm of Reynolds & King Brothers continues to expand their offerings adding drugs and proprietary medicines to their already burgeoning stock of dry goods, hardware, harness, saddles, groceries, provisions, grain, crockery, table-ware, and toilet articles.

The Denver & Rio Grande Railroad entices readers to spend their winter on the Pacific Coast. Special nine-month excursion tickets, costing $80 for a round trip, will whisk standard and tourist sleeping car passengers to California and the Northwest.

Porter & Obert of Delta enumerate nineteen reasons why folks should heat their homes with a "Buck's Hot Blast Heater." Buck's is a soft coal stove which is advertised to reduce coal bills by one-third.

J.C. Hart is looking into the proposition of starting a box mill if he can get enough associations and growers to use his boxes. The timber supply for making boxes is almost unlimited and easily obtained. Having a local box factory to pack apples and the like would put a supply always on hand. This year, boxes ordered from elsewhere in July did not arrive until October.

The Tongue Creek School lights a Christmas tree and gives a program. The Cedaredge School hosts a parents' reception just after Christmas. All parents and friends of the school are invited. Work by pupils is on display.

In Austin, Silas Rist consents to become a *Champion* correspondent. Another correspondent in Cory is hoped for. The Austin stone quarry needs more workers. Mrs. Delo's stone barn is progressing rapidly under the watchful eye of Mr. Brabbin of Cedar Mesa. The Earl Fuller house is nearly completed and Henry Schoenter has bought land and will begin building soon.

Little Ruth Blanchard of Cedaredge has been badly injured by a household accident. While playing with her sister, Ruth fell into a tub of scalding hot water. Before she could be rescued, one-third of her body was in a frightful condition. She has been hovering between life and death since the accident.

George Gipe, a well-known and respected resident of Cedaredge, dies suddenly while working at his ranch south of town. He appeared to be in his usual health, but a sudden heart seizure brought the end instantly. He is survived by two daughters, Essie and Lulu as well as sons, Victor, Harry, Ray, Leonard, and Guilford. Services are conducted on Christmas Eve at the Methodist Episcopal Church with interment in the new cemetery recently laid out southeast of the town.

In four years, since 1902, the profits of Colorado orchards have advanced by $100,000. For nearly two decades, Colorado fruit growers have not had a failed crop, whereas eastern states have experienced disheartening failures in apples and peaches.

A classified declaration by C.B. Pickett invites the parties who stole two razors from his residence on the day of his auction sale to return the same and nothing will be said. Otherwise, he promises, "I will expose the guilty parties."

T.W. Odem of Cedaredge notifies the public that a red, spotted steer calf has been staying at his ranch for some time. "I would," he says, "like the owner to come and get the same very soon." The animal has no visible brand although both ears are distinctively marked. Stockholders of the Young Creek Reservoir Company will meet after the first of next year.

A display advertisement submitted by Kennedy & Duffield's Subdivision asks, "Do you realize that the town of Cedaredge is rapidly growing in size? This means that the values of town property will not long remain at their present figures. There is no safer way to invest, nor easier means of making money than that of buying real estate in a prospering town. We invite you to inspect the lots in our sub-division, which you will find are admirably located and moderately priced."

W.A. Tim's Cedaredge Confectionery boasts a line of holiday candies, nuts and other sweet-meats. His store also features a bowling alley and pool room. The local mail schedule has conveyances leaving at 7 a.m. to reach Delta at 11 a.m. Mail leaving Delta departs at 4:30 p.m. and arrives in Cedaredge at 8:30 p.m. The Surface Creek Realty Company, managed by E.S. Corbin, invites residents to list property. The company also has money to loan on ranches and is set up to sell an irrigation user's surplus water.

Blanchard & Stockham announce a removal sale through the holidays to reduce their stock and make room for new spring goods. A sack of flour goes for $1.15 with good bulk coffee on sale for 15 cents. Seven bars of either Peacock or Diamond brand soap can be had for 25 cents. Corsets valued at $1.25 and $1 can be purchased at the reduced price of 75 cents and 50 cents, respectively. Night drawers, petticoats, knee pants, shirts, and hats range from 25 to 75 cents. Cash buyers will be able to purchase the foregoing goods at even lower prices.

A one-acre orchard on lower Surface Creek has a remarkable record in winning state fair prizes. Thus far, the same section has earned 1st place for Johnathan and Ben Davis apples, 2nd place for Winesap apples, and 3rd place for Grimes Golden apples. These accomplishments are apparently cited for example purposes only because no name or location is attached to the acreage.

James Zaninetti continues to encourage people to purchase lots in Cedaredge and the emerging town's immediate vicinity. The outlook for the coming year is strong. Land values have nearly doubled, yet the price of land remains low compared to other Western Slope districts. The population of the Surface Creek Valley has doubled to reach 212. More land has been cleared and planted in fruit. Local orchards have taken numerous prizes in commercial competitions. The coming spring promises to witness a large influx of settlers.

Christmas 1907

The *Surface Creek Champion's* dream of incorporation was realized in February 1907, by a vote of 62 for and 16 opposing. The crux of opposition was an unfounded rumor which led to the mistaken belief that the first order of business for the incorporated town would be the establishment of a saloon. The incorporation success seems to have inspired publisher Clyde W. Brewer because the December 1907 issues of the *Champion* are virtually bursting with news—both good and bad.

As Cedaredge approaches its first Christmas season as an incorporated entity, the entire community is united in mourning the tragic death of a popular young man. In early December, a fatal hunting accident takes the life of eighteen-year-old Cyrus Raber, the youngest son of Mr. and Mrs. Wm. Raber. Accompanied by his friend, Bertie Lane, Cyrus had been hunting rabbits three miles north of Cedaredge, on Thore Thompson's place, near the Lane home. On a chilly afternoon, around 4:30 p.m., Cyrus had run a rabbit into some rocks. The boys began digging on opposite sides of the pile when Bertie heard Cyrus' gun go off. He called to Cyrus but received no reply. Rushing around the pile and finding his friend badly injured, he ran for help.

Just how the accident happened can never be known, but it is probable that Cyrus had set aside his 10-gauge shotgun as he worked to dig the rabbit out. He may have slipped, bringing the gun up against his chin just as the trigger came in contact with an obstruction. As a result of these unfortunate events, the gun discharged causing injuries which resulted in instant death.

Neighbors carried the body to his home. His mother was stricken with grief. Word was sent to his father, who was working at the Grand Junction sugar factory, and the grieving father arrived the next day.

Cyrus was a student at Pannell School where he also served as trusted janitor. His kind and generous heart made him a favorite comrade among those of his own age and his faithfulness led adults to depend on him. He was a member of the Cedaredge Baptist Church where he served as president of his Sunday school class. In a front-page story, the *Champion* newspaper reported "The entire community was plunged into immediate sorrow over the tragic death of so fine and promising a young man."

On the day of the funeral, Cedaredge schools are dismissed at two o'clock and all pupils and teachers brave wintry weather to attend. In a stirring ceremony, the body of Cyrus Raber is laid to rest in the Cedaredge Cemetery beside the grave of his sister, Vida, who had died nine months earlier.

"Misfortunes," the *Champion* noted, "never come singly and the people of this Valley are a unit in extending to the sorrowing parents their heartfelt sympathy in this, their second sad bereavement during the year."

Author's note: Contemporary visitors to the Cedaredge Cemetery can view the weathered headstone which marks the final resting place of the Raber siblings. It is regrettable that, in the more than 100 years since these tragedies, the stone has weathered so badly that neither youth's name can be clearly discerned.

Winter weather spawns heavy snow and chilly temperatures, followed by a thaw which leaves dirt roads mired in mud, followed by another round of snow. Students have a difficult time reaching school. As a result, even faithful attendees are absent or tardy prior to the holiday break. The Grand Mesa receives even more snow. Tom Lund returns from a trip to Grand Mesa to report that the most recent storm deposited 2½ feet in the Leon Lake region.

Despite inclement weather, things are looking up because sidewalk construction is nearly completed. At present, only a very few lots are without walks and the town council has approved the purchase of additional lumber for sidewalk construction.

The new walkways are, the *Champion* declares, "an improvement which has added wonderfully to the looks and desirability of the town. Their full worth will be more fully appreciated when muddy weather arrives. The street crossings being put in by Marshal Dolph are worthy of favorable comment as he is certainly doing a good work."

Community spirit continues to coalesce around improvements. Several ranchers in the vicinity of Surface Creek Bridge have turned up to help the road overseer grade down the bad hill approaching the bridge on the lower side. This will greatly assist travel along that portion of the road.

Though snowy weather persists, a variety of Christmas programs are well attended. Filling Cedaredge Hall with laughter, young members of the Methodist Episcopal Church present a comedic performance with a moral message. A dozen actors stage the play "Which One Won?" Audiences pack the hall—adults paying 25 cents and children admitted for 15 cents. The cast includes: Daisy Richardson, Elmer Gipe, Mrs. Axa Mellor, Robert Douma, Earl Cronk, Lulu Gipe, Frank McCain, Marie Caldwell, Mamie Johnson, Roy Shinaman, William Melcher, and Arthur Boggs.

The Methodists also present a Christmas Day Sunday school program featuring a basket of candy and gifts and Cedaredge Hall hosts a Methodist reception. At a Baptist holiday gathering, Reverend J.R. George preaches on "The Spirit of Christmas" in morning, followed by an evening sermon entitled "Thoughts on Christmas Carols." The Baptists hold a Christmas Eve service. The order of events and participants are:

Song "Joy Bells" by the congregation
Prayer by Pastor
Duet by Ethel and George Humphrys
Recitation by Jessie Closson
Exercise "Christmas Songs" by ten girls
Ladies Quartet "At Midnight"
Recitation by Katie Gipe
Recitation by Arthur Ellison
Fairy Drill by twelve little tots
Recitation by Daisy Skinner
Trio sung by Mesdames George and Humphreys and Miss Humphrys
Recitation "Grandmother Gray" by Miss Avise

Christmas Wreaths by seven girls
Recitation by Jessie Skinner
Duet "The Babe of Bethlehem" by Misses Marie and Ruth Caldwell
Address by Superintendent
Recitation by Lucile Bolton
Recitation by Jamie George
Exercise "Flag Drill" by twelve boys
Tableau "Give Us God's Gift"
Distribution of Presents
Benediction

....

Author's note: Though the present-day Cedaredge United Methodist Church and the town's First Baptist Church occupy substantial structures, the early worship spaces for both denominations had humble beginnings. The location of the Baptist service described above is unspecified, but it was likely held in the church's large tabernacle—a sizeable and well-made tented structure erected in 1905. Prior to 1905, Baptists met in homes and various town locations. Situated near the site of the present-day brick structure, the Baptist tabernacle served the congregation until the current building was completed in 1909. Methodist services were first held in homes, then in a log structure, and later in Cedaredge Hall, which was erected in 1903 at a location west of the present-day town site. In 1915, the Methodists erected a large wooden tabernacle. In 1920, work began on the present-day stone structure which was completed in 1929.

....

The Eckert Glee Club performs at Cedaredge Hall with a holiday dance following the singing. The Women of Woodcraft will present a lunch social and entertainment at Cedaredge Hall on New Year's Eve. The program includes recitations, quartets, duets, solos, dialogues, and stirring readings. Topics include "The First Quarrel," "Ring Out the Old, Ring in the New," and "The Old Year Dies Tonight." On January 3, the season's first masked ball will be held at the Hall.

The Mound School at Cory provides Christmas Eve entertainment in the Eckert Hall, followed by a dance. Mr. Taylor, a Mound School teacher, boasts that the event will be the best of its kind ever held in the Valley. Tickets to attend the show are 25 cents for adults and 15 cents for children. Dance numbers may be purchased for one dollar.

Concerning schools, the *Champion* has offered to reserve space for news of the Cedaredge Public School. Each of the higher grades has elected a student to serve as editor. Ethel Humphrys is elected editor-in-chief. Lola Briggs will serve as ninth grade editor. Greeta Van Aken will be eighth grade editor and Ruby Hart will cover seventh grade. The lower grades will also submit news items as will students from the Pannell School.

Based on student editor reports, pupils in the highest grade have organized a literary society and appointed a committee to prepare bi-weekly programs. The eighth grade is studying stocks and bonds and they hope to complete their physiology unit by Christmas break and then take up civil government after the holidays. The ninth-grade class is three or four lessons ahead of Delta schools in the subjects of Latin and algebra. Seventh graders are studying geography. The physical geography class views a "Diminutive Volcano" created using chemicals for the eruption and an organ stool as a base. Observing student reactions, a school reporter sums up the experience by writing, "we imagine that it is as near as they ever wish to approach the beauties of Vesuvius."

Also at Cedaredge School, the school board has let out a contract for raising the belfry of the school house so that the sound of the bell will be heard farther than it is at present. The board is also seeking to have sidewalks laid along the south side of the school yard, with the length running even with the school house, then turning north to reach the stairs.

In support of science classes, a fine microscope is procured by Mr. Melcher at a cost of four dollars. "One glass," a student reporter declares, "magnifies an object fifty times its natural size, the other glass one hundred and twenty-five times. As yet we have had but one opportunity to test its worth. A tiny brown bug was placed beneath it and much interest was manifested by those who saw its increased size."

The student report continues, "We are all looking forward to the Christmas holidays and the two weeks' vacation promised by the board. A few are preparing to visit friends and relations at a distance, but the great majority are perfectly satisfied to spend their vacation in Cedaredge. There is plenty of snow for coasting and the ice is safe for those who like to skate. And then there's always dear old Santa to think about, and the good things mother knows to make. Hurrah for the fun! Is the pudding done? Hurrah for the pumpkin pie!"

Regarding skating, the *Champion* cautions that the reservoir in Harts Basin is frozen over in places and skating is good. "However, it is yet a little dangerous."

Author's note: The national economy also seemed to be skating on thin ice. The so-called Bankers' Panic in October 1907 and a similar panic in November continued to threaten national and local economies. The panics of autumn 1907 were precipitated by attempts to manipulate copper, coal, iron, and railroad stocks. President Theodore Roosevelt's trust-busting initiatives notwithstanding, big companies and daredevil investors were playing fast and loose with the stock market. Business failures and runs on banks mounted until the crises cooled. As Christmas 1907 approached, businesses and consumers may have been understandably nervous.

Despite the nation's economic jitters, the *Champion* discovers that Delta County businessmen, especially those in the City of Delta itself, "are very optimistic with regard to the present financial crisis. Many of them are preparing for the largest holiday trade ever had."

If the advertisements in December 1907 issues of the *Champion* are any indication, merchants in Delta and the Surface Creek Valley and elsewhere in the county were brimming with financial optimism.

New Surface Creek Valley advertisers include fledgling Cedaredge businesses. G.V. Fowler bills himself as a local auctioneer. Doctors Hadsell and Reed have set up shop in their shared residence which doubles as a drug store. Percy R. Devereux represents himself as an "up-to-date barber" who specializes in hair cutting, shaving, shampooing, hair dyeing, bleaching, and singeing as well as electric scalp and face treatments. Devereux also offers massage, hones razors, and acts as an agent for the Delta-based Steam Laundry Service. John H. Hartman will work as painter and paperhanger for cash or barter of a horse, spring wagon, plowing, or other services needed to operate a ranch. Johnson & James are contract builders and among the first to sign up for the new Delta County Co-operative Telephone Exchange, proudly listing their phone number as 11-X. And G.H. Webb's Fine Fruits—featuring berries in season and plants for spring setting—can be reached through the central operator by asking to be connected to Co-op Phone 7-M.

Veteran Surface Creek advertisers continue to purchase large display ads. The Cedaredge Hardware Company (precursor to the present-day Big John's Ace Hardware) offers the spectacular St. Clair Hot-Blast Heater at a reasonable price. Blanchard & Stockham's huge store suggests purchasing suits, shirts, and hats. Meanwhile, Davis Drug Company declares itself (in a possibly misspelled headline) "Headquarters for Santa Clause." The drug emporium also offers "Kodaks" another way of saying the company will snap and mount your photo because, "Nothing makes a nicer or more acceptable present than a kodak." The Davis Company further asserts, "Delta prices are given on all these goods. Trade at home and thus keep your money here. We have what you want."

Rival entrepreneur J.L. Sherd enumerates a wide array of holiday goods, in particular, gifts for children. The list includes drums and other musical toys; mechanical toys; toy banks; tops; as well as dolls and doll accessories. With every purchase of 50 cents worth of toys or other items, a customer will earn a chance to win "the prettiest doll in Delta county."

Author's note: Throughout the papers of the Champion, the names of companies and other entities, such as Delta county were written with the proper noun, in this case "Delta" capitalized and the descriptive noun, in this case "county," uncapitalized. Thus, Cedaredge's busy meeting place was described as Cedaredge hall as was Eckert hall. Schools were labeled Cedaredge school and Pannell school, etc. Surface Creek valley often appeared with valley in lower case. When company names appeared in display advertisements, Company was usually capitalized. However, when written in articles, the Davis Drug company and the Colorado Telephone company tended to appear with the word in lower case. In addition, when the shortened word for telephone appeared in print, it was abbreviated 'phone with a leading apostrophe.

In still other cases, as with the word Depositors in the paragraph below, words which ordinarily would appear in lower case were capitalized for emphasis. To give the reader a taste of the times, when quoting directly from the Champion text, the author has retained the vintage usage and displayed the excerpt as written. Otherwise, he has employed modern usage conventions.

Not content with mere newspaper advertising, Jas. K. Grant designs an attractive window display featuring good things to eat for Christmas.

The newly established Bank of Cedaredge boldly declares an "individual responsibility of owners" to the tune of $300,000 in assets. On-premises cashier, Joseph Hogrefe, asserts, "We offer absolute safety to Depositors and pay 5 percent interest on deposits. Lend your support to a home institution."

Under new management, the newly-reopened Cedaredge Hotel offers "excellent tourist accommodations, good table service, and comfortable rooms. Proprietor, J.C. Rowbotham offer special rates by the week and lists his co-op telephone number as 9-H.

Delta businesses are also well represented with large display ads. George C. Wilson is a manufacturer and dealer in saddles, harness, whips, and turf goods with hand-made goods his particular specialty. Geer & Clack provide a woodcut illustration of Santa Claus seated at a shiny new table with a caption which exhorts shoppers to "Buy Something Useful" such as furniture. "Our prices," they promise, "will interest the Christmas shoppers as well as those contemplating furnishing a house." Delta's H.K. Correll has just received a railroad car of furniture with another half a car on the way.

Buy Something Useful

So, the place is overstocked, inspiring the owner to sacrifice his heating stoves to make room. And at greatly reduced prices. In fact, downtown Delta appears to be overflowing with heating stove and range appliances. Porter & Obert, a firm which specializes in Buck's Stoves and Ranges, has these items available with "prices to suit." Finally, the Delta-based Grand Mesa Lumber Company, owned and managed by I.C. Hall, solicits the business of anyone planning to build, offering—among other items— lumber, nails, paints, oils, varnish, lime, and cement.

The Delta National Bank invites readers to "Bank by Mail If You Wish." Using this innovation, there is no need to come to town. A check from this or any other bank can be endorsed, placed in an envelope, and addressed to Delta National. "The mail will bring it to us and we will credit your account and mail you a receipt."

In real estate news, at least two large spreads are offered for sale: 40 acres 2½ miles northeast of Cedaredge and another 24 acres nearer town with 300 apple trees and also stands of blackberries and raspberries. Along these lines, County Surveyor, John A. Curtis, begins making an official survey as ordered by District Judge Shackleford. The work calls for re-surveying about 16 square miles of farmland lying east of Cedaredge—most of which is located on Cedar Mesa where controversy has recently arisen over property lines. T.N. Stevens of Delta and Abner McKee of Paonia are assisting Mr. Curtis. A petition prepared by land owners some time ago requested this survey to settle disputes arising from incorrect boundary lines. It is hoped the survey will "settle the matter for all time."

To entertain readers, the *Champion* launched a serialized feature in September. With publication of the continuing story reaching its eleventh episode in December, the marathon tale, "Hearts and Masks" by Harold McGrath, dominates page three.

Author's note: With illustrations and spirited dialogue, the "Hearts" serial can be compared to our modern-day romance novels. A national phenomenon, the series receives mixed reviews. The New York Telegram calls it "frenzied romance served hot in a piquant sauce of modernity." The Nashville American describes it as "a joy-spreading story that is spirited and swift in action." However, the Philadelphia Telegraph advises, "Take Harold MacGrath's story 'Hearts and Masks' with a grain of salt and simply enjoy it—there is no necessity of believing it, nobody wants you to!"

"What?" We Heard Him Exclaim.

In regional news, events taking place in nearby Olathe add further support to Cedaredge's decision to incorporate—an action which Cedaredge took in February 1907. Having also incorporated this year, Olathe held their first town election in late November and voted to move forward as a dry town by electing an anti-saloon ticket.

Eckert news flows in. Eckert has a new meat market. Chas. Hamilton is open for business in the Eckert Hall Building, just behind the James Dale blacksmith shop. Mr. Hamilton expects to supply people with fine beef and pork throughout the year. Subscribers to the Co-operative Telephone Company contribute money for the purpose of purchasing Christmas gifts to show their appreciation for the work of operators at the Eckert central office. Honored are Nellie Forest, Essie Jacques, and Della Lamar.

Concrete seems to be the medium of choice for new Eckert construction. Mr. Coffee is building a cozy concrete cottage on his ranch south of the Fairview School House. And, having sold 20 acres to reduce his holdings, John Kettle will build a concrete dwelling adjacent to his orchard. This particular building material also prevails in Cedaredge where E.E. Bull's concrete residence is rapidly nearing completion. Two stories high, the finished structure will measure 26 by 40 feet. Albert Stolte is engaged to do the woodwork.

Eckert hosts the annual meeting of the Surface Creek Ditch & Reservoir Company. The principle business is the election of officers and directors as follows: president Wm. Kennicott; vice president T.J. Harshman; treasurer Dr. A.E. Miller. These officers, together with H.W. Bull, Henry Hawker, J.R. Lamar, and W.R. Lyall, will serve as the company's board of directors. In other action, John Griffin is chosen as secretary. The meeting is unique in that some voting of proxies was received by telephone. The telephone being a relatively recent addition to Surface Creek, the phoned-in proxies are reluctantly allowed. However, it is decided that, hereafter, such proxies will have to be given in writing.

In other telephone news, a move is afoot to interest various reservoir companies in supporting the Grand Mesa telephone line. At present, the line is failing to meet expenses and, unless the reservoir interests take up the matter, the service will be discontinued. The service could end as early as this summer. Directors of the various companies will meet in the near future to discuss ways and means of extending the lines and continuing the service. In a related story, E.E. Leslie has traveled to Delta to supervise the work of establishing telephone connections between Delta County ranger stations. The U.S. Forest Service has initiated this project as a safeguard in the event of a sudden fire or other emergency related to the preservation of forests. Mr. Leslie and a crew of linemen will begin work as soon as weather allows. Similar work is being commenced throughout the Western Slope. It will take about three months to complete Delta County work before the crew proceeds to other areas.

Speaking of fire, fighting a modest blaze in Hotchkiss created a great deal of water damage. So much so, that the Duke, Deutsch, Scott Mercantile Company is holding a gigantic fire sale. The store's entire stock of general merchandise must be moved to make room for new, undamaged goods which have been ordered. The firm promises "unheard-of prices" for stock which includes $12,000 worth of boots and shoes and "a monster line of dry goods, clothing, and groceries."

In local personal items, cattle are on the move, by hoof and rail. John Shelledy drives the Hepworth cattle he's been feeding to Montrose and ships them to Kansas City. J.A. Whiting ships four stockcars-full of cattle to the Kansas City market and Jas. Buzzard ships two cars. Mr. Buzzard boards a train to follow the cattle.

Reverend J.R. George's New Year's topics to be presented to the Baptist congregation will be "Looking Forward" and an evening sermon on "Christ and Social Discontent." In addition to his pastoral duties, the reverend takes a hand in civic affairs. A special meeting of the Cedaredge town council is held for the purpose of approving bonds in support of Reverend George who has been appointed justice of the peace. Otto Peterson is arrested on a charge of carrying concealed weapons. The case is brought before Justice of the Peace George, who dismisses the entire affair.

J.P Kettle is acquiring rock for the foundation of his new house. O.P. Brookbank travels to Denver and returns with his young son who has been hospitalized for some time. The boy has been unable to walk and it was hoped some help might be obtained by taking him to see specialists in Denver, but the doctors there could do nothing.

A trio of Christmas weddings are announced. Chas. M. Cook weds Miss Jessie McCormick—both are Cedaredge residents. Jas. E. Beith of Delta and Miss Nora McGruder of Cedaredge exchange vows. H.R. Harrison and Miss Anne A. Buckly are united in marriage. The pair are new Cedaredge residents, the groom from Nebraska and the bride from Washington, D.C.

Working on Paynes Mesa, Mr. and Mrs. Wm. Miller and R.E. Griffith pulled and piled up about three acres of sage brush. Which worked up an appetite for a festive supper hosted at the home of Miss Caroline and Frank White.

M.J. Lane was badly injured in an accident at the Mellor Coal Mine when a large lump of coal rolled onto his hand and mangled his fingers. A set of standard scales have been placed at the Mellor & Easton Mine. The new scales will do away with the practice of using unsatisfactory guesswork to establish weight. The *Champion* is involved in the process by printing a large order of weigh tickets to be used at the mine. The price of coal from the Mellor & Easton mine is $1.75 per ton if obtained at the mine, or $3.50 if delivered to Cedaredge.

Lawrence McCafferty, formerly of Cedaredge, is seriously hurt in Ridgway. The nature of his mishap is not known, but he is not expected to live. Mr. and Mrs. J.L. Sherd are the proud parents of a baby boy.

Cedaredge Marshal Dolph is having trouble managing loose livestock in the city limits. When he attempts to impound a horse, the owners raise objections and serious trouble is narrowly avoided. Despite this incident, the marshal pledges the town ordinance covering loose livestock will be rigidly enforced.

The Elhart Brothers hardware store is installing a Standard Simplicity gasoline lighting plant in their place of business and also in Cedaredge Hall. This will greatly improve the Hall which has always been poorly lighted. Frank W. Childs has begun acting as agent for the Alabama Nursery Company which raises its own yearling trees for commercial orchards and guarantees delivery in perfect condition to Cedaredge.

Three Surface Creek youths are taken before Judge Dickerson in Delta on a charge of juvenile delinquency. The boys are in their mid-teens. Robert Woodward, Robert Dale, and George Buzzard are found guilty and placed on probation. The sentence is suspended in hopes their conduct improves in the future. However, if caught again in unlawful acts, they will be sent to reform school.

Author's note: Their offense was not specified in the December 1907 article. However, further research suggests that a September incident got the trio in hot water. Robert Dale was apprehended for throwing a rock which injured a woman who was being driven through town. Presumably his companions were also implicated. Young Mister Dale appears to have been something of a rebel. In 1906, he took a family horse and ran away only to be apprehended in Hotchkiss and returned home. Little else is known of Robert Woodward before or after his probation. As for George Buzzard, his story continues in Christmas 1919.

An update on the Gunnison Tunnel reports that the two headings (tunneling in intercepting directions) are within 8,244 feet of their meeting. As of now, the River Portal of the tunnel has surpassed 7,810 feet and the West Portal has achieved 14,462 feet.

The U.S. Forest Service is accepting bids for the construction of a three-room house to be used by forest rangers. The structure is to serve as headquarters for rangers during the greater part of the forest season. The building will be located on upper Surface Creek, approximately two miles north of the old Shelledy Camp. The building will adjoin 200 acres of land on which to pasture horses used by the Forest Service. A quantity of hay will also be raised nearby to feed the stock during the winter.

As Christmas 1907 draws to a close and a new year appears on the horizon, the *Surface Creek Champion* and its eloquent publisher, Clyde W. Brewer, remind Cedaredge residents to be welcoming to newcomers. His words are repeated here, just as they were written more than a century ago:

"The holiday season is a good time to remember the strangers among us. There are a large number of new families in Cedaredge to whom the Christmas and New Year festivities will bring memories of

old friends and old times and perhaps a streak of homesickness now and then. It is for those of us to whom Cedaredge seems the one and only place on earth, to include the newcomers in our thoughts and give them such a hearty welcome and greeting that they will forget, like the rest of us, that they ever lived elsewhere.

"There are several kinds of boosting. It is natural to think that once people have come among us and bought a home, they are sure to like it so well that they will want to remain among us as a matter of course. This would be so if their staying depended solely on the good qualities of the country itself; but this is not the case. If friends are not many and cordial, no place on earth seems desirable to most of us.

"There is therefore another and almost a more important kind of boosting, the making of people who have cast their lot here, so contented with social conditions that they will want to bring their old friends here to join them instead of longing to go back to old scenes themselves. Our town is in a transition stage of progress and many things are necessarily rather crude as yet in the making. We shall need the help of our new friends in making the community all that we wish it."

After relating an unfortunate incident of a rude resident astride a horse accosting visitors and driving them off a pedestrian sidewalk, the publisher continues his articulate plea for community civility.

"There are ten times as many people in Cedaredge and vicinity who believe in good order and good manners, as there are people who do not. All that is needed just now is for the people who are for the welfare of the town financially and its reputation at home and abroad, to combine a little and make their sentiments felt instead of letting a minority element such as is to be found in every town of any size, have things its own way.

"Here's a happy New Year to every new citizen of Cedaredge and the surrounding ranches, a year better than any one preceding in the history of the region, because they are with us and because we are still boosting for a better as well as a bigger Cedaredge."

Christmas 1908

Agriculture and water make front page news in the *Champion's* holiday editions. The water users of the Uncompahgre Valley are praised for action taken at an early December meeting in Olathe. Voting on the basis of water shares, the result is 74,052 for and 30 against amendments proposed by the Federal Government. "By this action, the completion of the great Gunnison tunnel is now an assured fact, and the work will be pushed to completion." The approved amendment calls for the current payment for water of $25 per acre to be enlarged to about $40 per acre—the increase needed to cover the cost of completing the tunnel.

In Eckert, a local movement is underway to install a waterworks. The plan is to lay a pipeline just below Cedaredge and run it the entire length of the Valley so that it can be tapped by farmers along the route. It is hoped that Eckert and Cedaredge can consolidate their efforts so as to carry the pipeline to a point well above Cedaredge with the goal of supplying the entire Valley with a good water system.

In crop news, despite the conventional wisdom that the most recent harvest was accomplished during a "crop failure year," estimates are that Delta County sold over $500,000 worth of apples. When sales of peaches, apricots, plums, prunes, and berries—as well as melons and vegetables—are added in, the aggregate sales will reach a million dollars. This amount does not include the marketing of $250,000 worth of sugar beets and the cutting of $100,000 worth of alfalfa, not to mention the raising of grain and potatoes and profits from large livestock operations.

Given these figures, the *Champion* asks: "Is there any wonder that Delta County is prosperous or that property values continue to climb?"

A word to the wise, however, that the almanac predicts a late frost for April 1909.

C.W. Brewer, who has variously described himself on the *Champion* masthead as publisher and editor, adds the title "proprietor" to his list of duties. The newspaper has now expanded to eight pages. Subscription rates remain $2.00 per year. Obituaries are printed for a flat rate of $1.00 but obituary poetry will cost an extra nickel for each additional line. A notice of thanks costs fifty cents. Advertising rates range from five cents per line to ten cents depending on whether an ad is plain text or headed and whether an advertiser is local or transient. If a church social, entertainment, or gathering charges admission and a profit is expected, ad rates apply. The *Champion's* policy is "no advertising of any kind done without adequate compensation." Meanwhile, Brewer apologizes for December issues being short of news. "The *Champion*," he declares, "does not contain its usual amount of news this week for two reasons, one is that there has been very little happening and the other is that we have been so busy attending to the wants of our holiday advertisers it has been impossible to get out and rustle much that has been happening."

Inspiring speculation about the Valley's future, a guest columnist who signs his work "A two-year resident of the valley" invites readers to turn their attention to the idea of building and operating an electric railroad connecting Delta, Cedaredge, and the upper Surface Creek Valley. The writer declares that there is little expectation that a steam railroad branch will be built since the Denver & Rio Grande Company care nothing about how far fruit raisers and others have to haul their products to reach the present railroad. Even if, after waiting for years, a branch is built, it would likely mean but one train a day. Whereas, "if we had an electric, we would be open to the outside world every few hours and in a short time could have a passenger service every hour from 7 a.m. until 10 p.m."

At present, branching out from Denver, electric rail lines are paralleling steam lines. Boulder, Longmont, Brighton, Greeley, Golden, and even tiny Leyden—while only a coal camp—all have electric lines which run passenger cars on the hour. To those in Leyden, a local electric line means a farmer who wishes to go to Denver can leave his team working in the fields, walk to the electric track, board a car, reach Denver in twenty minutes, conduct business, and be back on the farm inside two hours. This same benefit could be had by every farmer between Delta and Cedaredge.

Providing additional background, the writer notes that, in 1867, when Denver itself was not on the main rail line and the city wasn't prospering, Cheyenne, which was on the line, was thriving. Businessmen in Denver raised enough capital in three days to finance a rail line which was completed inside of a year. If Cedaredge, Eckert, Cory, and Delta—in concert with all the farmers in between—took hold of the same spirit which had transformed Denver, the Valley could have an electric railroad in time to ship next year's fruit and sugar beet crop.

An electric line would also increase property values and the expense of such a line would be nominal. Electricity could be generated by water power; not only to run the railroad but to supply farms and towns along the line with electric lights. Furthermore, electric power would only be needed to haul the empty cars up the Valley, whereas loaded trains could travel most of the return distance by gravity.

In church news, the men of the Baptist Church have organized what will be known as the Baptist Brotherhood. The object of the brotherhood is to take up the work of the Y.M.C.A. as an extension of church work. Officers elected by the 15-member brotherhood are: Will Sturdevant, president; Fred Gibson, vice president; Lester Seaton, secretary; and W.G. Davidson, treasurer.

The Sunday School class of the Methodist Episcopal Church is hoping to "provoke one another unto love and good works" by encouraging punctual attendance. In a recent contest, girls earned 43 points for punctuality and the boys only managed 29. A Methodist reception gathers fifty people to welcome the new pastor. Reverend and Mrs. J.S. Ferris are treated to a literary and musical program. F.A. Briggs welcomes the new pastor on behalf of the church and C.S. Blanchard represents the Sunday school. Refreshments of cake, cocoa, and coffee are served.

The Young Women's Christian Temperance Union (YWCTU) holds a song service at Cedaredge Hall. Reverend J.R. George gives the address "Why Sign the Pledge?" whereas Reverend Ferris speaks regarding "Is the influence of the drunkard worse than that of the moderate drinker?" Songs and discussion round out the evening.

Christmas services are held in the new Baptist Church building. While the building is not yet completed, it is made comfortable for the service. The men of the congregation clean up the premises and, as the windows have not yet arrived, canvas is stretched across the openings so the room can be heated. The new church is rapidly nearing completion.

Holiday sermon topics include "Waiting for Santa Claus" and "The Christmas Spirit" at the Cedaredge Methodist Episcopal Church. Baptists will explore "The Spirit of Christmas."

At the Cedaredge School, the 8th grade has completed their history studies and will be reviewing their lessons before the holiday break. That grade's present challenge is to draw the eye and ear, which they are finding quite difficult. The same may be said of the 8th grade's study of Latin, Greek, and English prefixes and suffixes. The 7th grade is studying the Revolutionary War and will next tackle the geography of the exotic South Sea Islands and Australia. Grammar school pupils have their picture taken—a group photo of everyone. A pre-Christmas debate keeps the grammar school engaged. The debate question is, "Resolved that railroad transportation is more important than (nautical) navigation." Navigation is declared the winner. Debate officers are Elmer Morris, Bernice McReynolds, and Delia Scott.

Cedaredge students welcome the return of Arthur Cobbett who has been absent for some time with whooping cough. Professor Melcher's room has improved heating. The stove has been moved nearer to the chimney, dispensing with many lengths of pipe. The stove is also enclosed in a galvanized jacket which causes heat to be more evenly distributed throughout the room. As of November, enrollment stands at 163 with an average daily attendance of 144. Thirty-seven students were marked tardy and 82 pupils were neither absent nor tardy. Seven high school pupils have been neither absent nor tardy during the previous four months: Susan Cook, Luella Davidson, Greeta Vanaken, Mary White, Leah Webb, Mable Webb, and Maud White.

News from the Eckert special correspondent finds that the community orchestra is doing well. The orchestra consists of the following: violin played by Elmer Jarvis; piano, Mrs. Cliff Hopson; first cornet, Louis Cesprini; second cornet, Herald Jarvis; clarinet, Frank Luellen; and drums, Cliff Hopson. At their Christmas dance, the orchestra introduces a new feature which goes by the name of "moonlight waltz." They will also play for a New Year's Dance.

Also in Eckert, Reverend McGlashan has returned to town to assist with Baptist Church revival services. Dr. Walker, whose family will relocate to Grand Junction, held a successful moving sale. The Eckert box social has been postponed indefinitely. George Warhing, an old and respected resident who is numbered among Eckert pioneers, died of pneumonia. Margarite Forrest narrowly escaped injury in a horse and wagon mishap. Her father, Richard, had hitched up a team to take the little girl to school. Passing through a gate, he'd gone back to close it when the horses ran away. Luckily the team was caught and halted and the wagon did not turn over.

A singing school is organized in Eckert under the tutelage of Professor Wright of Maine. Mrs. Helen Beckley is thrown from a horse but sustains no serious injuries. Walter Johnson suffers several cuts and bruises when horse and rider have a fall.

A Tongue Creek pioneer passes away after battling an illness brought on by a poison oak infection. Henry Pomtier had settled in the area in 1887. Having reached the age of 46, he is survived by a wife and son. Funeral services are held at Eckert with burial at Eckert Cemetery. In more cheerful

Tongue Creek news, the school house hosts a Christmas program and deco-
rates a tree.

T.W. Odem of Cedaredge announces that a three-year-old heifer with
a white face and distinctive ear marking along with an unbranded yearling
steer have wandered onto his ranch. The owner of same is asked to retrieve
the animals immediately. Otherwise, they will be advertised as strays. Meanwhile, several animals have strayed including two short yearling steers and a
bay gelding both bearing distinctive brands.

*Author's note: Beginning in 1906, the office of the Colorado Secretary
of State published a comprehensive Colorado Brand Book which was
not only a volume of much interest and public importance, but also
what one newspaper called "a mechanical curiosity" because of the way
the book was printed. The challenge of producing a book of brands was
legendary since most livestock brands amount to creative combinations
of letters, numbers, shapes, and lines which do not lend themselves to
being printed from the raised letters of a typical printing press. The
problem being that the letters, numbers, etc. used for livestock brands
are often manipulated in nontypical ways. For example, a brand for
the Lazy 4 Bar Ranch might consist of a numeral 4 lying sideways (that
is, being lazy) with a single line representing a bar above, below, or
to one side of the misaligned 4. The standard raised type of a printing press cannot accurately reproduce hundreds of unique brands. To
the rescue came a printmaking methodology which had been used by
artists for centuries. Planographic printing means printing from a flat
surface, as opposed to a raised surface. This method of printing is based
upon the idea that water and oil do not mix. To create a planographic
print, a metal plate or stone surface is covered with a greasy substance,
but desired letters, numbers, and shapes are left ungreased so that those
elements are receptive to ink while the greased surfaces reject the ink.
Early versions of the Brand Book were printed in books small enough
to be carried in a rancher's or farmer's pocket. These days, the Colorado
Department of Agriculture administers approximately 30,000 registered Colorado livestock brands, therefore modern Brand Books are less
portable, although their contents are readily available on-line. The Department emphasizes that brands are a permanent mark on the hide
of an animal and that, to function as an indication of ownership and
a "return address," a brand must be registered with the state Brands*

Division. Tattoos, ear tags, and microchips may be useful, but they are not recognized as brands. To view the singular nature of hundreds of Colorado livestock brands, visit the Delta County Libraries and ask to check-out one of their many Brand Books.

In other crop news, Alfalfa might be considered a coming commodity. The selling price of $3 per ton has risen to $5, with the prospect of going as high as $10. And yet, stock fed on Surface Creek hay always seems to bring the highest prices in the cattle market. So, perhaps local farmers should stick to hay.

In a round-up of local news, H.W. Bull has leased his ranch for the coming year to Amos and Elmer Gipe who will take charge in the spring. Mr. Bull will continue to reside at the ranch, but he'll be attending to other matters, including taking a sight-seeing trip in the near future. C.M. Hocker has leased his hay ranch west of Cedaredge to I.W. Utterback for next season. Mr. Hocker expects to devote his entire time to his large cattle interests. He's finding it too much to manage both hay and cattle. Carl Odem and Earl Turner each killed large bobcats. These animals seem to be very numerous this winter.

"Don't Smoke," an article urges. "I am not much of a mathematician," said the cigarette, "but I can add to a youth's nervous troubles. I can subtract from his physical energy. I can multiply the aches and pains. I can divide his mental powers. I can take interest from his work and discount his chances of success."

Two homes are under construction in the Cedaredge area. Chas. Springer is erecting a neat little four-room residence on his lots in the west part of town. C.W. Alexander completes a small residence on the 20 acres he recently purchased from R.W. Curtis.

The Delta-based H.K. Correll enterprise is moving to a new store which has prompted a huge display advertisement touting a "Great Removal Sale." His inventory includes furniture, rugs, and ranges.

GREAT REMOVAL SALE

Advertiser Phil Stephens does precision surveying and Dr. R.E. Mehaffey provides dentist services during the first week of each month. L.C. Bolton's physician and surgeon office is open in a location opposite the bank. Working out of Lovett's Barn, C.A. Dowdy guarantees his veterinary services which includes a pledge that, if directions are followed and no cure is made, no charge will be made. His specialties are ring bones, splints, spavins (arthritis of a horse's hock or ankle), and all diseases of the foot.

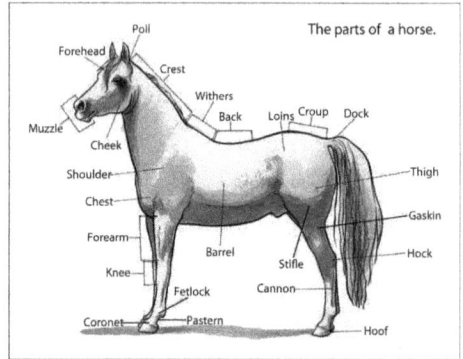

The parts of a horse.

Poll, Forehead, Crest, Withers, Muzzle, Back, Loins, Croup, Dock, Cheek, Shoulder, Chest, Thigh, Forearm, Gaskin, Barrel, Stifle, Hock, Knee, Cannon, Fetlock, Coronet, Pastern, Hoof

G.A. Hawkins offers a holiday spruce-up with first-class barber work. W.J. Brabbin deals in hay, grain, and feed in his shop south of Cedaredge Hall. The Surface Creek Co-operative Coal Company is now in full operation selling an abundance of clean and well-screened coal at $1.60 per ton. O.P. Brookbank is the coal operation's superintendent. Jas. Stell of Eckert has installed a siphon on the Co-operative mine to carry off water which has been encountered. The location of the mine makes such an arrangement feasible and it is believed there will now be no further trouble with the water.

Sherd's store offers the most complete line of outing flannels on Surface Creek with prices ranging from 7½ to 12½ cents.

Author's note: An "outing flannel," according to other sources, is a soft and lightweight cotton fabric or twill tweed with a short nap, or flapped cover, on both sides—primarily worn by infants. No word on how the half-cent will be collected.

Sherd's has gone all-out this year with festive window displays. One window contains a lavishly decorated Christmas tree with a Santa seated near it. The store hopes to attract customers by giving away a toy automobile in which a boy or girl can ride.

In classified ads, H.C. Getty offers pigs for sale. Cedaredge Meat Market offers sour kraut and bulk pickles. David Lyall is selling cheap one acre of land adjoining the west side of the school ground. The Hillman store's annual clean-up sale may mean that no child in this county need go without a winter coat for Christmas—$2.50 will buy a choice of any one of 25 garments. W.S. Grant will be much obliged if the party who borrowed a pickaxe two weeks ago will return it. Using a term which might be more recognizable in Canada, W.H. Forrest and Phil Westen are both advertising for sale a "milch cow."

Author's note: Though it may appear to be a misprint, the term "milch cow" was commonly used in the early 20th century to describe a cow raised and kept for her milk. Its origins may stretch as far back as the early 15th century. Its presumed root—which it shares in common with emulsion and milk—means to rub off or to stroke—apt descriptions of the motion used to hand-milk a cow. In addition to dairy applications, the term is sometimes used to describe something easily obtained or taken for granted. The fairly modern idea that the middle class is "the milch cow of government" suggests that class of individuals is seen by government as an easy touch for political power, money, consensus, etc. The idea bears some resemblance to calling someone or something a "cash cow." Recent immigrants may have been more likely to use the term milch cow or milch kine. The term kine (another word for cow) appears in the Bible, for example, and in vintage ballads like "She Moved through the Fair." Suffice it to say, rural folks living in 1908 knew and used milch cow and milk cow more-or-less interchangeably.

The post office store offers magazine subscriptions, post-card albums, and hundreds of new Christmas and New Year's cards, not to mention Christmas candies in attractive boxes. Apparently acting as a collection agent, the Bank of Cedaredge holds unpaid coal bills owed to the Co-operative Coal Company. Grant's Blacksmith Shop suggests that farmers who want work done should not wait until spring because it is nearly impossible to keep up with demand during that busy season. Broken machinery, dull plows, and the like should be looked to now.

Residents are encouraged to shop locally. Prior to Christmas, Cedaredge merchants will remain open evenings in order to accommodate holiday shoppers. J.K. Grant installs at his general store a Dayton computing scale which he maintains is the very best upon the market and absolutely accurate in every way. Grant is a bit nervous about Christmas because some of the goods he has ordered especially for the holiday have not yet arrived. In any event, Grant is keeping up his Christmas spirit by having Santa Claus on hand to distribute holiday treats including bananas, oranges, dates, figs, nuts, and cranberries. Cedaredge Hardware hopes to interest husbands in purchasing one of their new White sewing machines for the busy wife or mother. Reynolds & King Brothers of Eckert offer low prices and courteous treatment while selling everything needed by the farmer. Blanchard & Stockham offer nuts and candies for Christmas.

The Cedaredge Drug Store has toys, stationary, and pyrography (woodburning) sets. As a holiday inducement, the drug store will give away a beautiful doll. "The doll," the store promises, "is one of the finest we have ever seen and a chance on it should be the desire of every little girl in the country."

Remington-Elliot's shop asks and answers the age-old question, "What would a man prefer for Christmas?" Answer: Something useful which he himself really needs, but thinks he cannot afford, such as: a new hat, suit, overcoat, tie, hosiery, gloves, suspenders, mufflers, slippers, house-coat, or umbrella.

A rail carload of fencing and barbed wire has arrived in Delta.

The Evans Mine (formerly known as the Landreth Mine) offers good coal. Located on Dry Creek, the Evans outfit offers coal at $1.50 per ton if obtained at the mine, or delivered anywhere for a reasonable price.

Weather in the Surface Creek Valley has been stormy with heavy snow turning to warm rain. The roads are in fearful condition. A combination of rain and snow has spoiled the ice on the Cedaredge skating pond. The stormy weather is widespread. Word comes from Denver that the city has experienced the heaviest snowfall in years. A weekend storm dumped a foot of snow causing traffic to come to a standstill.

Although more snow is in the forecast, the Bank of Cedaredge suggests saving for rainy days. And, as the holidays approach and the desire to keep in touch with distant relations increases, the Colorado Telephone Company reminds readers that they can say 450 words in three minutes. Which comes in handy when using the company's toll line because the three-minute out-of-town rate is very low. The team of Sanford and Stone, representing the rival Co-operative Telephone Company passed through Cedaredge on their way to Coalby. Their intention is to gauge the interest of Coalby residents in connecting to the co-operative line. The people there have a small system of their own, but have no outside connection.

In seasonal society and club news, after several years of planning, the Masons are organizing a lodge. A hall is the main consideration and a meeting of sixteen members have decided to remodel the Eckert Hall by making improvements consistent with laws governing the order, including deadening the floor.

Author's note: Deadening the floor appears to be a quaint way to describe carpeting a wooden floor to make it more-or-less soundproof. A common practice when a meeting hall, as in this case, is a floor above someone who does not wish to be disturbed by upstairs noise.

In other club news, the Woodmen of the World hold a grand ball on Christmas night at Cedaredge Hall.

Author's note: The Woodmen of the World (aka the Modern Woodmen of America) is a national fraternal and benefit society founded in the late 1800s. Originally established as a group which looks out for its members by providing financial assistance and other means of support, the modern organization has merged with other groups and evolved into a financial services enterprise which provides life insurance to members as well as annuities, securities, credit union services, and gravestone markers. There are currently an estimated 2,000 lodges in America.

Fred Byrd has gone to Iowa and it is rumored he will not return alone. The same rumor of not returning alone is attached in reverse to Chas. Taft who is expected home from Tincup for the holidays. Several Christmas-time weddings are scheduled. Miss Emma May Alexander will wed Clarence Eugene Vanaken. Miss Marie Winifred Caldwell will become the bride of John DeWayne Hugh. "There are," the *Champion* adds, "rumors of others which cannot be stated as certain."

Mr. and Mrs. Martin Peterson are the proud parents of a fine baby boy. Miss Ethel Avise entertains thirty people at the home of her parents. The gathering is held in honor of Mr. and Mrs. Louis Griffith, newlyweds who are spending their honeymoon with Mr. and Mrs. Avise, who happen to be their grandparents. Mr. and Mrs. Hart of Hart's Basin are recovering from a recent illness. Alex Lyall has departed for his former home in Scotland. He expects to sail from New York and arrive in Pultney Town, Scotland, in time for Christmas dinner.

In apple news, H.J. Baird of Delta is off for Iowa, to attend the National Fruit Congress. He carries with him a fine collection of apples from Delta County along with a number of pamphlets advertising the area. Reporting back at Christmas, he declares that he displayed 50 plates of apples and distributed 4,000 pamphlets. Delta was the only Colorado county which appeared at the Fruit Congress.

J.B. Hart of Hart's Basin boasts one of the largest and finest orchards in the country, but this year he suffered considerable losses from a spring frost. He will be prepared this coming spring to smudge in a thorough manner if it becomes necessary. Hart had ordered smudge pots and will need to obtain in the vicinity of 50 tons of coal. At present Hart is experimenting with different types of coal. Using a Cartright and Archer pot, he finds that 16 pounds of Co-operative coal will burn for four hours and 20 pounds will burn for five hours. Twenty pounds of Sommerset coal burned for more than seven hours. However, given the cost of coal, the local brand is cheapest, so that will probably be his choice. Hart is continuing to experiment with his next strategy being to test different brands of pots. More data is coming in since J.G.A. Simpson has been testing the Olson coal pot at Redlands Ranch. The *Champion* suggests other orchard managers follow the lead of Simpson and Hart in order to be prepared for the possibility of spring frost.

Author's note: Smudge pots are oil-burning devices used to prevent frost on fruit trees. The pots are generally round with a chimney. Burning oil creates not only heat and smoke, but also carbon dioxide and water vapor. With modifications, pots are still used today along with orchard wind machines mounted on lofty towers. Retired wind machines can be viewed along Surface Creek Valley's main highway—Highway 65. The machines are on display at Cedaredge's Pioneer Town and at Fritchman Orchards in Eckert.

W.S. Nelson has returned from California where he saw evidence that Colorado apples are besting the competition. Delta County Jonathan apples of a less than superior grade were being sold for $2.50 a box whereas California apples were going for 75 cents to a dollar per box. And yet, so long as Colorado apples were available, even at a higher price, California apples were not selling. Upon visiting California fruit producing regions, Nelson found thousands of boxes of apples on the ground going to waste because there was no market for them.

A visitor from Illinois arrives to spend time with Pete Koppenhafer on Young's Creek. The visitor is looking over the country with a view of locating a number of families here, all of whom are good farmers.

A professor from the Agricultural College at Fort Collins is anxious to hold a short course in methods at Cedaredge as soon as satisfactory dates can be arranged. It is hoped arrangements can be made for the course to be given this winter.

A meeting of the newly formed Surface Creek Improvement Association would, the *Champion* feels, go a long way toward making the upcoming year "more of a hummer." The newspaper also maintains, at Christmas, everyone should be happy and, if there are any who have experienced misfortune, it should be the duty of every citizen to make his burden as light as possible with acts of kindness and charity. This should be true all year round, but especially during Christmas.

A perennial concern which distresses the *Champion* is jealousy among Western Colorado towns over where the legislature ought to locate a state normal school (teacher training college). There are no colleges on this side of the Rocky Mountains and Gunnison is the present consideration where an ideal site has been donated and the state has already invested in improvements. Gunnison may have disadvantages, but what town does not? the *Champion* asks. The newspaper urges "people of the slope" to cease disagreeing and support the Gunnison site. "Unite," the paper suggests, "and accomplish results, divide and accomplish nothing."

Just before Christmas, the *Champion* shares an article in which the nearby *Delta Tribune* has kind words for the Surface Creek Valley. The area has, in the *Tribune's* opinion shown much development within the last three years, with 1908 being the most remarkable. The upper Valley has produced a full crop of fruit together with an enormous production of hay, grain, berries, beets, and tomatoes. Cattle interests have also added to the prosperity. Many families have relocated to the Valley in the past twelve months and many comfortable homes are built or underway.

Continuing its glowing assessment of the Surface Creek Valley, the *Tribune* reports that large fruit companies, backed by eastern capital, are buying up old cattle ranches and sagebrush lands which they are converting to fruit operations. Some 200,000 trees were set in orchards last year. Hundreds of railroad cars of fruit were shipped to all corners of the nation. Valley homeowners own their own co-operative coal mines from which they get a good supply and good quality of coal. The coal business is under the efficient management of A.W. Hall and Chas. Rowell. Two high schools were opened in the Valley last year. All leading to a 20% increase in land values.

Concerning individual towns, the *Tribune* notes that Cedaredge boasts two new churches and no saloons. Austin has enlarged its packing houses and canning factory. Eckert is alive with newcomers.

The *Champion* relishes praise from a brother publication, but reminds readers that a trip to Delta is sufficient to recognize that the Surface Creek Valley needs better roads. In many places, the center of the road is so low that water stands and makes mud so deep it is almost impassable. In other places where a road should be found, the traveler encounters a row of sagebrush or stumps. The new county commissioners seem to be road enthusiasts, but if area farmers and local merchants can work together, the Valley might yet have roads and highways worthy of the name.

Christmas 1909

As the holidays approach, the promise of a glamorous prize and a whirlwind trip to Denver inspires local residents. Photographs are a rare luxury in early copies of the *Surface Creek Champion*. Nevertheless, a December issue features an image of a fashionable prize which awaits the yet-to-be-chosen queen of the first Colorado National Apple Exposition. In a full-length front-page black-and-white photo, a model appearing in the display window of the Denver Dry Goods Store wears a $200 gown and $75 hat which will be awarded to the new Apple Queen. In addition to stylish clothing, young women selected to compete for the title will receive railroad fare to Denver and a hotel stay in the city during the Exposition from January 3-8, 1910. All candidates will enjoy entertainments including theater parties, banquets, and automobile rides. Only one queen will be chosen. Other representatives will be Maids of Honor and each will receive a token of the occasion—a celebratory ring to be presented by the Colorado Governor himself.

The *Champion* encourages Surface Creek supporters to vote for a young miss of their choice. Coupons printed in the newspaper are to be used as ballots and single votes can be increased by purchasing or renewing a newspaper subscription—at the rate of a vote for every penny. For example, the $2.00 purchase of a yearly subscription entitles the subscriber to cast 200 votes for the candidate of choice. Also, *Champion* advertisers offer enhanced votes in exchange for purchases. Other newspapers in Delta County and elsewhere in the state also seek to enlarge votes to elect a queen candidate while also boosting subscriptions and commercial sales.

The contest is set to end on Christmas Eve. As the local competition draws to a close, the *Champion* seems blissfully unaware of the firestorm of controversy which the battle for Apple Queen is destined to kindle. The first hint of drama in the Surface Creek contest emerges when two young ladies— Miss Harriet Luellen and Eva Stell—ask, without giving reasons, to have their names withdrawn. Hettie Rist, Esther White, Iris Kennicott, Minon Kennicott, and Mary Simmons garner only a few votes each and, as Christmas Eve draws near, those five names are dropped, reducing the local field to three contenders.

When the votes are tallied at 6 p.m. on December 24, 1909, Miss Edith Blanchard emerges as Surface Creek's representative, compiling an astonishing total of 95,674 votes. Miss Lola McHugh places second and Miss Ina Odem finishes third. The *Champion* urges local residents who plan to attend the Denver Apple Exposition to "do all in their power to boost the Surface Creek candidate in order to honor the valley as well as the candidate."

Across Colorado, several newspapers and communities launch their own homegrown contests. The competitions are spirited and, eventually, twenty-five young women receive a free trip to Denver. It is evident that Miss Blanchard makes the journey because she publishes, in the January 14, 1910, edition of the *Champion*, a public letter thanking her supporters for making the trip possible. Miss McHugh also thanks her supporters and makes the train trip to assist the Surface Creek winner and stand ready to take the winner's place if needed. Although Exposition promoters have made no provision for second-place candidates, from the outset of the local contest the

Champion had pledged to provide transportation and $10 in expense money for the Surface Creek runner-up. However, the newspaper was adamant that absolutely no voting coupons from other newspapers would be accepted in choosing local representatives.

Ultimately, Miss Blanchard is not chosen to reign as Apple Queen. That title is bestowed upon Miss Mabel Skinner representing Fruita, with Delta's Genevieve Hartig placing second and Excie Cady of Paonia finishing third.

Author's note: Taken at a festive ball held at the Brown Palace Hotel in Denver, the January 1910 photo below is part of the Denver Public Library collection. It did not appear in the **Champion.** *Queen Mabel Skinner of Fruita is shown in the near center wearing an obvious crown. Somewhere in this vintage photo is Edith Blanchard serving as a Maid of Honor and Lola McHugh, the Surface Creek Valley's runner-up, may also be pictured. Each Maid received a commemorative ring presented by Colorado Governor J.F. Shafroth. Two such rings—including one which belonged to the Apple Queen representative from Olathe—were donated to and have become part of the collection of the Stephen H. Hart Research Center at the History Colorado Center in Denver. A rough count of those pictured who appear to be Maids, plus the chosen Apple Queen, yields the twenty-five total which most newspapers report as the number of representatives sent to the 1910 contest.*

The Denver voting is marred by controversy. The voting was to have taken place with Exposition admission tickets used as ballots—one ticket, one vote. But a last-minute scheme is devised to allow individuals to purchase additional votes. It is also alleged that balloting was cut short prior to the 10 p.m. deadline. These concerns will lead to revised procedures for future contest elections.

Author's note: Another concern is the sheer number of Apple Queen contestants. The original idea for the contest called for each Colorado district—ideally in places where apples are grown—to be given an opportunity to elect a representative to the Exposition. Newspapers in apple districts were called upon to carry out the contests by publishing voting coupons which could be clipped and filled in with a name. Unfortunately, the notion of state apple districts in 1910 was a matter of conjecture so that some young women might have been chosen from towns and regions which are not necessarily known for apple production. Also, some newspapers as well as businesses, had taken the idea of enhanced voting to extremes, raising issues about impartiality and fairness.

In the end, Colorado embraces its new Apple Queen. Although neither of Grand Junction's two candidates had been chosen, the city nevertheless rolls out the red carpet for the victorious Fruita representative, welcoming Miss Mabel Skinner as visiting royalty. The Apple Queen contest of 1910 will be remembered for its feisty competition and flawed voting process. But the contest also spawns a pair of enduring Colorado legends in the form of a hometown hero and a young woman who chose love over glory. To impart the details of those legendary stories, it is necessary to cite Colorado newspaper sources beyond the **Champion.**

On New Year's Eve 1909, it is reported in the **Aspen Democrat** *newspaper that Miss Mamie Gray, recently elected Apple Queen representative from the Hotchkiss district, "proved herself a heroine when she rescued four people from death. At 1 o'clock, fire broke out in the home of Thomas Gregory and Miss Bray not only entered the burning building in time to assist Gregory, his wife, and two children to safety, but the young woman went to the fire station and with several volunteer firemen helped pull the hose cart to the scene and later took charge of a line of hose." (As for the accuracy of this story, the Aspen newspaper didn't specify a.m. or p.m. and Miss Gray's name is misspelled "Bray.")*

On Christmas Eve 1909, as reported in the **Montrose Press,** *the* **Olathe Criterion** *newspaper lost one of their leading candidates for Apple Queen when Miss Mintie Kirks threw over her chances of winning by choosing to marry Mr. Hague W. Dreon of St. Louis. In an article written in mock protest, the Criterion declares that Miss Kirks' large number of friends felt she had "a royal chance of being chosen Apple Queen from Olathe. She prefers, however, to shine as the queen of a household rather than as a regal representative of a common industry like apple culture."*

A further note regarding the second- and third-place finishers in the voting for Surface Creek Apple Queen representative. In May 1910, Miss Lola McHugh went to work as a Cedaredge telephone operator for the Colorado Telephone Company, a post she resigned a year later upon her marriage to Charles Kiser. Miss Ina Odem was an accomplished musician and popular young woman whose father, T.W. Odem presided as president of the local school board. The elder Odem and his son Carl operated Red Mountain Ranch—a conglomerate of orchards north of Cedaredge. The spread produced peaches, apples, plums, prunes, apricots, cherries, mulberries, grapes, and almonds. Far from lamenting her loss in the queen contest, Miss Odem hosted a party of twenty young people where, it seems, her brother Carl and Miss Blanchard, the reigning Surface Creek Apple Queen, made a charming couple. Fast-forward to September 1910 and Odem-Blanchard nuptials united Carl and Edith in marriage. In 1917, Miss Ina Odem married C.A. Pollard and moved to Norwood in San Miguel County. In February 1919, news reached Cedaredge that Ina was ill with influenza. Her mother arrived at Ina's bedside just a few moments before the 27-year-old, former candidate for Colorado Apple Queen breathed her last.

Not to be outshone by the Apple Queen contest, preparations for the National Apple Show also call for Delta County to contribute sufficient apples to make up a carload on the special Boosters' train which will run to Denver for the occasion. The Denver & Rio Grande Railroad has promised the county will have access to "the finest train the road can procure, so that boosters can have a comfortable trip." Reduced rates will be granted.

Tickets for the Delta County Special go on sale December 20. The journey itself will take place on Sunday, January 2. The train will leave Paonia at

3:45 p.m. Departure time from Hotchkiss will be 4:25 p.m. The train leaves the Austin station at 5:15 p.m. and departs from Delta at 6 p.m. After making stops at a few larger towns along the route, the train is scheduled to arrive in Denver at 7 p.m. on Monday, January 3. The roundtrip fares to Denver are as follows: from Paonia $21.15; from Hotchkiss $20.65; from Austin $19.80; and from Delta $19.40. The Pullman fare to Denver is included in the price. Pullman fares for the return trip will be charged at regular rates. About 150 people from Delta County are likely to ride to Denver and growers are encouraged to bring along extra boxes of apples and literature to distribute along the route. Among Surface Creek growers planning to ride the train, is Jas. Stell of Eckert. Mr. Stell is particularly looking forward to the Denver Apple Show since the festivities will also include a buffalo hunters' reunion. Stell serves as secretary of the reunion group.

In other apple news—involving actual apples—the *Champion* reports that G.H. Webb's entries of local fruit in the Washington State apple show have earned a first place and two second place awards. Furthermore, Delta County and Surface Creek apples have dominated prizes awarded at the Iowa-based National Horticultural Congress. Out of 42 entries, county exhibitors garner 36 prizes. And, of those three dozen honors, Surface Creek captures 30. Surface Creek winners and their winning apples are:

> **Henry Hawker** for winter apples, *Rome Beauty, White Winter Pearmain, King, Smiths Cider,* and *Grimes Golden;*
>
> **J.A. Luellen** for a single standard packed box and *Spitzenburg;*
>
> **Dr. A.E. Miller** for *Rome Beauty, White Winter Pearmain, Lauver, Yellow Newton, Jonathan,* and *Gano;*
>
> **G.E. Williamson** for *Mann and Greening;*
>
> **E.E. Bull** for *Champion, Stark Special,* and *Senator;*
>
> **L.A. Dowds** for *Winesap;*
>
> **J.B. Ratekin** for *Yellow Bellflower;*
>
> **J.B. Phronie** for *Ben Davis;*
>
> **George Dyer** for *Huntsman;*
>
> **John Wetterich** for *Greening;*
>
> **H.F. Thomas** for *York Imperial;*
>
> and **C.P. Nutter** for *Fameuse.*

Things are looking up for apples, but there appear to be a few rotten ones. Uncovering a shocking lack of Christmas spirit, two new arrivals to Delta County disclose that they paid $2 for a box on the Chicago market which was marked "Delta County fruit" and labeled "Fancy." Opening it, they found a layer of good apples on the top and another such layer on the bottom. But, in the middle of the box were a large number of under-sized, worm-eaten apples. The specimens were "wholly unfit for eating and so bad that a self-respecting farmer would be hesitant to offer them to his hogs." Evidence suggests that the mislabeling and dishonest packing is not an exception because the same men bought a box labeled "Delta County Fancy" in Denver with the same result. In light of these shocking revelations, the *Champion* urges local growers to prevent such shoddy boxes being placed on the market. "If these packs are allowed to go out, it will be but a short time before it will be hard to dispose of our products." The goal of all area orchardists should be an honest pack for local apples so that the words "from Delta County" on the box is "a guarantee that the goods inside are perfect and an invitation to the buyer to *come again*."

Appealing to honest orchards, the Colorado Fruit Growers' Association, managed by W.P. Dale, offers crates, Larson fruit ladders, Bowman picking bags, and spraying materials. Early ordering of materials is recommended in order to spray to prevent black leaf. Box shooks—bundles of wooden parts to be assembled into fruit boxes—should be ordered early lest the grower find themselves faced with a "box famine."

Surface Creek Fruit Growers Association, whose fruit house is located at Austin, announces that, in addition to handling fruit, they will handle flour and stock salt on a wholesale basis. Austin has a railroad depot and a great deal of freight hauling for the Valley comes through that location. As a result, and owing to the shorter haul, merchants and growers will make a saving.

Recent shipping figures reveal that Colorado leads all Western States in fruit shipped and that Delta County leads the state in apples. Colorado shipped a total of 4,300 railcar-loads of apples with Delta County accounting for 2,000 of those carloads. Washington State was Colorado's nearest competitor with 1,740 carloads of apples. And yet the combined total of apples shipped by Washington, Utah, Idaho, Montana, Oregon, and New Mexico fell 800 carloads short of the amount shipped by Colorado alone.

In livestock and ranching news, J.B. Killian's cattle which are raised and fattened on Surface Creek have won recognition of a high standard at the Chicago Stock Show. Killian himself is back in the county and looking after some cattle who are still out on Grand Mesa. He reports the snow about 2½ feet deep at the site of his summer camp.

Readers are warned to beware of a scheme designed to cheat farmers and ranchers. So called "lightning rod sharks" and "barbwire fiends" prey on unsuspecting customers. Barbwire frauds are on the rise. A salesman offers a contract to erect an 8-wire fence at eight cents per foot. If the customer signs, he discovers too late that he's agreed to pay eight cents *for each wire*. For an average job, a farmer has to surrender his farm in part payment and give a note for the balance.

The State Agricultural College at Fort Collins will conduct a one-day institute for farmers. Lectures on agriculture and horticulture given by professors from the college will take place in Cedaredge after the first of the year.

In coal news, Chas. Daniels has been pushing work at the States Coal Mine north of Cedaredge and he's discovered a vein. Charles States had earlier worked the mine which bears his name from the south side, but water had forced him to abandon the workings. States then prospected lower down and on the north side, but efforts were unable to locate the vein until recently. A drainage tunnel has been driven in and a drill sunk down to reach the vein. The drainage tunnel should handle any water at the new workings.

The *Champion* reports that December 1909 opened with cloudy skies and dry, but very chilly, weather. As of December 3, "Not much snow has fallen in the valley, but up in the mountains several feet (of snow) have been added to the already good supply. While a little disagreeable at this time, it brings assurance of big crops next season." In Cedaredge, the mercury dips to eight degrees below zero although it is much colder in other parts of the state, including Delta, where one report sets the low temperature at minus 27 degrees.

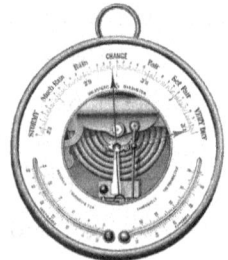

After a spate of extremely fine weather, followed by the "coldest spell of the season," a big Christmas Eve storm drops a load of winter moisture. The snow reaches a foot deep and still the snow continues. The Valley is treated to a "real old-fashioned snow storm" which lasts for several hours, adding another five inches. Those with sleighs and skates welcome the storms. The young folks are making the best of it by coasting for fun down various grades and steep hills. Sleighing is not confined to the young as everyone who can find a pair of runners is taking advantage of the snow. Several Cedaredge young people are tempted by snowstorms to take a sleighride to a dance in Delta.

Bad weather is likely to hamper building operations in Cedaredge. E.H. Woodard is hoping for fair weather now that the town council has granted a permit to build a small frame building facing Cedar Mesa Street. The new structure will be located next to the Cedaredge Hotel and will be occupied by Mr. Woodward to set up his harness shop.

The *Champion* is of the strong opinion that two new pedestrian crossings are needed in Cedaredge. On 2nd Street, a rock pile serves as a crossing and this unsatisfactory situation should be cemented or planked as it is a disgrace to the town. Another crossing is needed to travel across Cedar Mesa Street from 2nd Street. A crossing at this location would serve people who wish to reach the post office when coming from the eastern part of town. A trip to the post office in muddy weather requires the public to make a detour of nearly half a block in order to cross the street. The town council should resolve this matter before muddy weather sets in next spring.

Author's note: Modern readers should be aware that what was known, in 1909, as Cedar Mesa Street is now Main Street. What was once considered Main Street is now the pathway occupied by the modern-day pavement of Highway 65. Also, the 1909 post office was not in its present location and there is some debate as to what was considered 2nd Street in 1909.

News out of Austin suggests wintry roads are getting a bit better. Everyone is busy preparing for the Holidays and the Denver Apple Show. Excavating work has begun for the settlement's new Methodist Episcopal Church. A new house being constructed for J. Runnoe is nearly completed and it promises to be one of the finest homes in the Valley. J.M. Lobdell and Holly Miller are also making plans to build this winter.

In Cedaredge School news, the library is moved from the grammar room to the high school room to make more space for seats in the grammar section. Lee Rowell enrolls as a high school pupil. An organ has been temporarily placed in the high school room and those who pass at noon or during recess are likely to hear a concert. Tressie Lovato had to return home after getting rock dust in her eye. Miss Morse will substitute for Miss Hosterman who will take the teacher examination in Delta. The fifth graders paint the relief maps which they molded last week. J.F. Walsh, of the upper end of the Valley, is appointed to the position of president of the Cedaredge school board. The appointment is made by the county superintendent to fill the position left vacant by the departure of Mr. Odem. Myrtle Collins quit school on account of the family moving to Cedar Mesa. This event leaves an enrollment of 43 pupils in the grammar room.

At Cedar Mesa School three new pupils are expected since Alvah Welch and family have moved into the Dry Creek neighborhood.

It has been said that three marks of modern convenience are the telephone, rural free mail delivery, and good roads. These are slowly emerging in Surface Creek Valley where two telephone companies compete to offer service and rural free delivery reaches from Austin to within three miles of Cedaredge. However, good roads are lagging. As holiday mail increases, the area Rural Free Delivery (RFD) carrier announces that he has passed the 2,000-mile total of his year-long journey to deliver the mails. Arthur Blake has put in three days hauling rock and sagebrush to fill the mudhole between Albert Lowel's corner and John McKinnon's place. McKinnon and Lowel deserve credit for turning out to help when the road was impassible for the mail carrier. Reporting on events along his route, the carrier notes that Ed Cole's fine black mare has died. Mr. and Mrs. Geo. Winters have moved into their new house and erected a mail box with a properly marked route number.

In other RFD news, the carrier reports good sleighing from Flint's to Rowbotham's. E.A. Bowers has a new mailbox up. Some big ditches are becoming clogged beneath bridges which is flooding the roads with ice and water. Mrs. Mary Sturdevant has purchased property in Cedaredge so she now expects to get her mail in town. The carrier will be at his office each week on Thursday, Friday, and Saturday evenings—excepting holidays—for anyone who needs to pick up packages. For stamps and money orders, the carrier will accept checks, providing they are good.

In Tongue Creek news, one holiday accident appears likely to lead to a fatal end and the other results in escape from death by a narrow margin. Recently injured in a horse runaway, L.R. Blake sustains internal injuries and can live but a few days at the most. Blake's accident occurred near the Fred Burritt Ranch. Better fortune attended local resident William Dowd's accident in Silverton. He fell a distance of 90 feet, was hospitalized, but is likely to recover.

An accident at the Somerset Mine has killed Joe Cesprini, a former resident of the Surface Creek Valley. The brother of Eckert resident Louis Cesprini and an acquaintance of James Zaninetti of Cedaredge, Joe Cesprini is laid to rest in a service preached by Reverend Cox of Cedaredge. He is buried in the Eckert Cemetery.

A mid-December cave-in at the Co-operative Coal Mine hindered the work of getting the coal out. The company had been excavating a section of the mine to create a working room when, overnight, the roof of that room caved-in. No injuries were reported but, since no other room was available, a double force had to be put on to create a new entry and turn out a new working area. As a consequence, there is now a shortage of coal.

Tuberculosis, resulting from many years spent mining, has claimed the life of Jeremiah Ryan. He died at his ranch north of Cedaredge. His remains will be laid to rest in the Cedaredge Cemetery. A committee of the Cedaredge Camp Number 681, Woodmen of the World expresses their condolences in a resolution of respect signed by L.M. Closson, F.W. Childs, and J.L. Patterson.

In Cedaredge, W.S. Gorsuch considers himself a lucky man. He had been hunting near his home "when his repeating shotgun refused to work owing to a damp shell. In trying to force the shell in the chamber, the gun was discharged within a very few inches of Mr. Gorsuch's face. Six inches closer and the full charge would have lodged in his chin and jaw."

Fred Frank of the Valley meets with a holiday accident while coming down from his ranch. Near town, one of the front axles of his buggy broke, throwing him out and under the conveyance. Fortunately, he escapes with nothing more serious than several scratches and a few bruises.

J.S. Wright has returned from Kansas City where he has been seeking medical aid for his young son. He is optimistic that the treatment his son is receiving will improve the boy's condition, though it is still early days in the procedure. Mrs. Wright and the boy will remain in Kansas for several weeks.

Holiday classifieds advertise fine hats by Mrs. Shinaman. No word on whether she will carry the Turban Style Hats which the *Champion's* fashion and patent medicines page touts as the latest thing. Mr. W.F. Shinaman will weigh heavy produce such as hay, grain, and potatoes at a cost of ten cents. The Shinaman's have opened a new Cash Bazaar in the store formerly occupied by E.H. Woodward. They offer Christmas gifts, notions, household items, and other handy articles. The store has a full line of holiday goods and notions at right prices. As for Woodward, he was obliged to go out of business on account of an inability to secure another building. He will likely spend the winter in New York.

In support of local merchants, the *Champion* declares that "From the looks of the Holiday stocks now being opened in Cedaredge it will be unnecessary to send or go elsewhere for the good you will need during the Christmas season. Buy at home and thereby build up your own community. Cedaredge is one of the busiest little burgs in the country these days. The merchants all report a big business aside from preparing for Holiday trade. It is anticipated that business in the Holiday line will exceed any previous year."

In anticipation of the demand for Christmas presents for smokers, Brown's Confectionery has stocked a very fine line of pipes of all grades. The shop also carries a line of cigars in five- and ten-cent grades put up in Christmas boxes. The confectionery is also running a holiday contest. With each 25-cent purchase, a shopper can guess how much money is in a glass jar. The lucky guess wins the jarful in an announcement set for Christmas Eve.

Grant's Store offers fresh buckwheat flour as well as sheepskin lined coats, work shirts, and whip-cord and corduroy suits, plus hogs for sale at the Stockham Ranch. Grant's is also running a holiday contest through January 1. For every dollar in cash, a shopper will earn one chance to win a lady's or gentleman's gold watch by the Elgin Watch Company.

Sherd's Store carries cranberries and wool blankets to keep warm during cold nights and the proprietors remind shoppers to return their Meteor coffee sacks to decide who will be awarded the Christmas bonus of a percolator coffee pot. Sherd's Store has the latest jet-black decorative trimming buttons on hand and Santa is due soon. Winners of giveaway contests sponsored by Sherd's are Ed Harris whose lucky ticket number 915 won a silver tea set and Leon McCormick whose 1011 ticket won a beautiful child's doll.

W.J. Brabbin at the feed store is selling one horse weighing 1,200 pounds and one span of young mules. Roy A. Downs is willing to part with 10–15 shares of Leon Lake Ditch & Reservoir stock.

Gale Patterson, president, and R.P. James, secretary, announce that stockholders of the Lone Pine Ditch & Reservoir Company have an extended time to subscribe for increased capital stock of the company. The new deadline is January 1, 1910. Stock not subscribed will be offered for public sale at $200 per share—which cost can be paid in fourths between January 1910 and July 1911.

Give Satisfaction

Blanchard & Stockham's new store advertises Thoroughbred Hats which "give satisfaction. We have 'em in all Shapes and Sizes." The huge store is operating a Christmas give away of a baby's bear skin coat and bonnet with chances given for each fifty-cent purchase.

Author's note: The original Blanchard & Stockham building remains in its historic location at 205 West Main Street in downtown Cedaredge.

A.L. Frost offers guaranteed services as a plasterer and contractor who specializes in tile work, concrete work, and masonry. A. Blake of Cedar Mesa advertises alfalfa for sale, "20 tons of third cutting, fine for milk cows. Will deliver any quantity. Also 80 tons of first and second cutting in the stack." G.T. White has established parlors next door to the post office to ply his trade of undertaking and embalming. He can be reached at Co-op Phone 18-G. Dr. Harry A. Smith has taken rooms 12 to 18 in the new Delta-based Stockham building. From this location he will visit Cedaredge monthly to provide services for the eye, ear, nose, and throat. Those who miss him prior to Christmas will have to wait until January 7 of next year.

"Does your machinery break down? Do you need extra help? Do you have sickness in the family? Have other emergencies arisen?" If so, a holiday advertisement declares, you need the assistance of the telephone—a message from the Colorado Telephone Company. A competing firm, the Cedaredge line of the Co-operative Telephone Company, has subscribed thirteen new phones. In Eckert, a similar co-op adds nine new phones on the line.

In Cedaredge, co-operative telephones are placed in the residences of Phil Stephens and E.D. Smith. The office of R.W. Curtis, Mrs. F.E. Brown's confectionary, and W.S. Grant's blacksmith shop have received co-op telephones. C.H. Dillon, G.A. Morris, and W.J. Myers have had co-op instruments installed as have the ranches of E.E. Frost and A.L. Frost. Meanwhile, a bad fall on the sidewalks of Delta injured Mrs. D.R. Stanford, the mother of R.L. Stanford of the Co-op Telephone Company.

THE TELEPHONE PLEDGE

I BELIEVE IN
THE GOLDEN RULE
AND WILL TRY TO BE AS
COURTEOUS AND CONSIDERATE
OVER THE TELEPHONE AS IF
FACE TO FACE

Author's note: The Colorado Telephone Company and the local Co-op Telephone Company were competing for Cedaredge customers. Co-op operators, women who answered as "Central" before routing calls, worked in a compact building which is still standing at 140 SW 2nd Street in downtown Cedaredge.

The telephone is a new device to many and only a few local residents have the instrument in their home. As a public service, the *Champion* newspaper publishes periodic reminders regarding telephone etiquette.

Apparently striving to reach a compromise between the local Co-op Telephone Company and the Colorado Telephone, the *Champion* lists both phones on its masthead: Co-op 'phone number 18-L and Colorado 'phone number Delta 77-3.

The Davis Drug Store hopes to increase holiday sales by attracting customers with an Apple Queen offer. The store has acquired 2,000 votes to cast for an Apple Queen representative and they will let the public decide which candidate will receive this bonanza. Each 25-cent purchase at the store entitles the shopper to one vote for the young woman of their choice. The woman receiving the most in-store votes will earn the 2,000 votes. This honor goes to Miss Edith Blanchard, who ultimately wins the post of local representative to the Apple Queen competition.

As a Christmas gesture, Manager Rowbotham of the Cedaredge Hotel is distributing 1910 calendars as well as wall pockets to his patrons.

Author's note: A wall pocket is a vase-like receptacle with a flat back and made to hang on a wall.

It may be winter, but a *Champion* cartoon evokes memories of summer with a couple in a canoe. Meanwhile, land sales are brisk. E.S. Corbin, manager of the Delta-based Surface Creek Realty Company, dubs himself "The Pioneer" and an expert on water rights. Corbin, whose references include any Delta County bank, invites readers to write for literature, transportation, and price lists. His prime listing for Decem-

CERTAIN DEATH.

Hilda—Would you lay down your life for me?
Harold—Glady, dearest.
Hilda—Then go and tell father of our engagement.

ber is a nice level 20-acre valley ranch two miles from town. His real estate rival, R.W. Curtis, takes a larger display advertisement with the large headline: "Improved Ranches and Orchards." Curtis declares that "Inquiries are coming in for some well improved places around Cedaredge and Eckert. If you have something along this line, come in and list your property. I am here for business."

During the second week of December, real estate transfers in Delta County reached a single-week total of $125,414. Among the beneficiaries of this surging market is J.B. Lazear who arrives from Hotchkiss to close a deal for the sale of his ranch north of Cedaredge.

Virgil Atchison is the local agent for Singer Sewing Machines. He's also managing the post office and his Cedaredge shop has received a new holiday shipment of rugs and window curtains to augment his already complete stock of furniture. Where furniture is concerned, he declares customers can get just what they want. However, he warns, "One month later the piece you want may be sold to the early buyer." And, with father and mother in mind, the store offers fine rocking chairs with prices ranging from two to eighteen dollars.

W.G. Little, proprietor of The Cottage Hotel offers good meals and comfortable beds for holiday visitors at reasonable rates. J.L. Patterson is now the proprietor of the Cedaredge Pool and Billiard Hall with a connected bowling alley. He advertises his enterprise as "A clean, quiet place of amusement. Fine cigars, candies, and tobaccos always in stock." Before Christmas, however, Patterson sells his business to Wayne and Bub Ives who will come up from Denver to take charge of the place.

With winter roads presenting a challenge, the Cedaredge Hardware Company declares, "This is the time of year you are in need of GOOD Buggies and Spring-Wagons." The local hardware carries the Winona brand of wagons, buggies, and spring-wagons with "every rig guaranteed to the limit."

As of November 16, 1909, The Bank of Cedaredge holds deposits of $82,323.18—a substantial increase from their starting point on February 14, 1908 when deposits totaled $21,868.72. Among its resources, the bank lists $50,363.61 in loans and discounts. After a brief illness, Roy A. Downs is back at work behind the counter of the bank.

In society and club news, December dances are scheduled for Cedaredge Hall and a holiday dance takes place at the Coalby Hall. Eckert Hall plans a New Year's dance. A Grand Christmas Ball is held at Cedaredge Hall. A three-piece orchestra furnishes the music. The trio is composed of Mr. and Mrs. Parker and Dr. Aust. In support of the grand ball, Mr. Rowbotham serves up a turkey supper at the Cedaredge Hotel. Tickets to "the swell affair of the season" go for $1.75 per couple with the hotel supper included.

The local Rebekah Lodge enjoys a social evening of games and other forms of amusement. Holiday punch and Nabisco's are served. The Modern Woodmen of America's regular meeting at Cedaredge Hall is announced by the group's clerk, Roy A. Downs.

The Odd Fellows have elected new officers for the coming year. John McKinnon will serve as Noble Grand. L.E. Dolph is Vice Grand. Will Kiser is secretary and Glen Elhart takes the role of treasurer. An oyster supper is served to seal the nominations.

Author's note: The reader may have noticed that oysters were often served as part of Surface Creek Valley celebrations and meetings. What was the attraction? A 2017 blog posted by Mari Isa of the Michigan State University Archaeology Program shares research which holds the answer. During the late 1800s and early 1900s, oysters, which had previously been harvested by hand, were being hauled up in great quantities using dredges and iron mesh bags which fishermen dragged across the ocean floor. The resulting harvest placed as much as 160 million pounds of oyster meat on the market each year. The exploitive harvesting did irreparable damage to the ocean environment, but it also created an ample supply which meant oysters—compared to beef and other options—were relatively cheap. High availability and low cost made oysters a popular option for rich and poor alike. Eating oysters was also trendy and considered sophisticated. Stricter food handling regulations, the connection between contaminated oysters and typhoid outbreaks, and prohibition eventually diminished the popularity of oysters. Why was prohibition a factor? The closing down of saloons and bars, where oysters were a common side-dish, led decreased demand and by the mid-1920s oysters were out as a go-to food.

In other news of local activities, Mrs. Cora Buzzard hosts a meeting of the Young Women's Christian Temperance Union. The first meeting of the Coalby Literary Club results in the election of Frank Fickes as president; B.F. Yeoman, vice president; Mrs. Warren Parker, secretary; and Chas. States, treasurer. The question up for debate which will be commenced when the club next meets is: "Resolved, that there is more happiness in the world than misery."

The Midland Jubilee Singers appear at Cedaredge Hall and the demand for tickets for the holiday concert may create a crowd which is far in excess of seating capacity. In order to accommodate season ticket holders, single night reservations have been temporarily discontinued.

A Christmas wedding is in the cards for Miss Virginia Elizabeth Gorsuch and Mr. Raiff Clair Nelson. The site is the Dry Creek home of the parents of the bride.

In church happenings, a new organ arrives for the Cedaredge Baptist Church—a very fine one of the Hamilton make. The Ladies Auxiliary of the Baptist Church hold an apron and homemade candy sale at the church. A pie social is held in conjunction with the sale and women and girls of the congregation are asked to bring a pie with the owner's name on the bottom of the plate. A gentleman will choose the pie he likes best and pay based on the weight of the owner at the rate of 25 cents a hundred. The event nets $25.

The success of Baptist activities was tempered by the resignation of Reverend W.H. Cox. The Reverend will depart in February.

The ladies of the Union Sunday School stage an entertainment and erect a Christmas tree. Dr. J.A. Johnson of Delta gives a holiday talk at the Methodist Episcopal Church. His lecture is based upon Edgar Allan Poe's "The Raven." Dr. Johnson finds deep meaning in Poe's writing. The talk is suitable for adults and children who will be admitted, respectively, for 25- and 15-cents.

The Mormons are holding services in the Tongue Creek school house.

News out of Eckert reports that skating at the Basin Reservoir has been very good. Meeting in Eckert, the Surface Creek Ditch & Reservoir Company chooses officers and directors. Tom Harshman is president and J.R. Lamar will serve as vice president with John Griffith filling the role of secretary. These officers together with H.W. Bull, John Young, J.O. Simpson, and Mr. Dorlan compose the board of directors.

Elsewhere in Eckert, C.M. Hopson is improving his place by building a large barn. Mrs. Belle Hanson's new four-room cottage near Eckert is completed. Chas. Hamilton and John McHugh return from Kansas City where they have been marketing several railcar-loads of cattle. C.P. Hopson leaves for Chicago where he will complete his studies in the College of Anatomy, Sanitary Science and Embalming. He will return next year in the spring to be with his parents during the fruit season.

Two accidents leave Eckert residents bruised and battered. John Kehmier slips on the ice and falls, suffering a broken collar bone and bruised head. Mr. Jacques sustains injuries by being stepped on by a sharp-shod horse. He is rapidly recovering.

L. Mason Lee, secretary of the Cedar Mesa Ditch & Reservoir Company announces that the annual stockholders meeting will move from the Lee Brothers Ranch on Cedar Mesa to the Delta office of Porter Plumb. The question of separating the ditch from the reservoir is discussed and officers for the ensuing year are elected.

John Shelledy, president, and H.K. Ferguson, secretary, of the Park Reservoir Company announce the company's annual meeting for the purpose of electing new officers. The group meets in Eckert.

R.W. Curtis receives an early Christmas gift in the form of a mounted deer head and a similarly preserved cinnamon teal duck. Curtis shot the deer himself some time ago near Paonia. The duck was shot by Percy Devereux. Nevertheless, Curtis purchased it to add yet another trophy to his numerous mounted specimens which he highly prizes.

In a festive display ad, the *Champion* extends to its readers and friends the Season's Greetings. "We thank you for your kindly treatment in the past and hope the New Year may find us better able to merit your friendship. We now wish you a Merry Christmas and a Happy and Prosperous New Year."

Christmas 1910

Imagine padding downstairs in pajamas on Christmas morning—heart racing and mind brimming with anticipation—longing to unwrap one special gift which must surely be under the tree. Now, imagine opening that long-awaited package only to find that the contents don't quite live up to expectations.

Surface Creek Champion proprietor and editor Clyde W. Brewer may have experienced a similar let-down upon receiving unofficial notice of the results of the most recent U.S. Census. Conducted in April 1910, the 13th annual census of the United States yields mixed results for the Surface Creek Valley.

Author's note: Beginning in 1790, a census had been conducted every ten years and, until the late 1880s, Western Colorado wasn't much of a factor. Even when lands formerly inhabited by Native Americans were opened to non-indigenous settlers, Western Colorado—and particularly the Surface Creek Valley—were mere blips on the census radar. The insistence of cattlemen, farmers, and miners who saw opportunity in the land had been gaining momentum, but the opening of ancestral native lands became inevitable following the Meeker Incident (as described in this book's Christmas 1906 chapter.) In 1881, when the Ute People were expelled, non-natives lost no time in populating the land. That year, the Denver & Rio Grande Railroad begin laying tracks from Gunnison to Grand

Junction. In September 1881, even as the Utes were being displaced, their land was being surveyed and sectioned. By Christmas 1881, the area's population was growing and the region was poised for expansion.

Despite the area's controversial history of conflict and forced removal, by 1910 the Surface Creek Valley has experienced, in a few decades, a meteoric rise from a sparsely populated land to a booming agricultural region—a dramatic transformation which should be reinforced by the census. Therefore, the 1910 census figures, though preliminary and perhaps disappointing to some, are front-page news.

The government has not yet released official Western Slope census numbers, but enough is known to inform readers of preliminary statistics. The 1910 census figures focus on the growing town of Delta and Delta County in general. Also highlighted are Mesa County and Grand Junction, along with Montrose County and the Town of Montrose. Here are the figures reported by the *Champion*, their accuracy being subject to confirmation from other sources:

According to unofficial census data, Delta County's population in 1910 is 13,560, a 150% increase over the 5,488 total gleaned from the 1900 census. The City of Delta's population was 816 in 1900. By 1910 the city has grown to 2,363 souls. Grand Junction's population, as measured in 1910, increases by 121% to total 7,755 and Montrose has more than doubled from 1,287 in 1900 to 3,264 in 1910.

Clearly, the populations of Delta County and its Western Colorado communities are steadily and dramatically increasing. The denizens of the Surface Creek Valley have contributed to this growth even though the 1910 census totals don't include discrete numbers for individual Valley communities. The *Champion* does its best to report on the results, but the structure of the census makes for an imperfect view.

According to the *Champion*, "The figures for Cedaredge are not obtainable at this time, but the precinct total (for the upper part of the Surface Creek Valley) is 1,291. Precinct 4 or the lower part of the valley below the Trickel bridge shows a population of 1,253. The figures for the previous census (in 1900) cannot be had, but the increase has far more than trebled especially in the upper precinct."

Author's note: By 1910, the Surface Creek Valley had been divided into upper and lower portions with each area considered a "precinct." As is the case in modern times, these precincts were essentially political in nature, that is—using population densities as a guide—they were established as a means to nominate candidates for public office and a way to organize voting. Where smaller communities were concerned, the 1910 census apparently focused on political precincts. In August 1910, the Champion *published a 733-word explanation of the legal boundaries of Surface Creek Valley Precincts 4, 7, and 16. The August article described, in excruciating detail, the section, township, and range of each precinct—with so much specificity that it is more instructive to summarize, rather than reproduce verbatim, the details. Suffice it to say that Precinct numbers 7 and 16 refer to different sections of Cedaredge and the town's vicinity. Those living in Precinct 7 voted at the Hadsell Building; those in Precinct 16 voted at Cedaredge Hall—which may suggest a roughly east/west division. Residents of Precinct 4 voted in Eckert. Included in the historic Precinct number 4 were the towns of Eckert, Cory, Austin, and Orchard City.*

Though some may consider Orchard City a recent phenomenon, the name goes back to 1912 when it was attached to a loose incorporation of Austin and Orchard City. When the concept of forming a consolidation of the communities in the lower Surface Creek Valley gained traction in the 1980s, it was discovered that Eckert and Cory hadn't been officially annexed. A considerable sum was invested in public notices to rectify the annexation oversight and, ultimately, Orchard City achieved a sense of unity. Even so, locals—especially long-time residents—continue to refer to their location by the name of each town and persist in considering themselves residents of one of the amalgamated communities.

As an enthusiastic booster of Cedaredge, Publisher Brewer may have wished to emphasize to readers that his beloved town was growing. He states that the town's population has grown three-fold in the passing decade, but does not cite specific figures. Undoubtedly, between 1900 and 1910, the town population would have increased. However, one interpretation of the 1910 census figures might be that the combined population of towns in the lower reaches of the Surface Creek Valley was comparable to the population of Cedaredge. That Cedaredge would one day become the most populous and prosperous of the bunch was, in 1910, far from a certainty. Eckert, Cory, and Austin were closer to the Denver & Rio Grande Railway line—especially Austin which possessed freight loading sites and a passenger station. The three communities were also closer to Delta, the county seat and emerging county population center. For that matter, the burgeoning communities of Paonia and Hotchkiss were also situated on the rail-line and these two communities had their own issues with the census. They disputed the 1910 census figures which reported Hotchkiss as having a population of 600 and assigned Paonia a population of 1,007—totals which the citizens and city fathers considered to be gross undercounts.

In other local matters which transcended the census, an idea that had appeared in the *Champion* in Decembers 1905 and 1908, seems to be gathering steam—or rather voltage. The notion of an electric railroad operating from Montrose to Delta and on to Cedaredge is still progressing. The proposed route would involve both Montrose and Delta Counties and, the newspaper declares, "it will be but a short time until the matter will be before the people of the two counties." A December meeting in Delta includes folks from Montrose, Delta, and the Surface Creek Valley. Local men present are: Roy A. Downs, B.F. Elhart, Phil Stephens, and R.W. Davis. Mr. Paret, who's described as "a prominent railroad contractor of Kansas City, offers "to do the preliminary work of making plats, securing right-of-way and bonus, (and to) dispose of the bonds and put everything up to the time of actual construction in working order. To do this a fund of $7,500 must be raised all of which would be required for the work."

Author's note: Stating the worth of 1910 dollars in today's terms is a tricky calculation. By some estimates, $7,500 in 1910 would be equivalent in purchasing power to around $235,272.63 or let us say about a quarter of a million dollars. This presumes a price increase of more than 3,000%. In other words, $7,500 in 1910 was a lot of money.

An additional electric train meeting is held in Cedaredge wherein Mr. Paret together with Mr. Sprague of Montrose and Mr. Bruce of Delta again outline the plan. According to the *Champion*, "The plan, in short is to name 25 men who will put up sufficient funds to carry on the preliminary work.

These men were to be divided between the two counties with one from Denver." The goal in Surface Creek Valley is to find six men "who will shoulder their share of this preliminary work and the prospects are good that they will be found. More definite plans will be announced later." With the holidays, nothing especially new is expected to develop, but the *Champion* reports that "prospects are very bright. The preliminary sale of stock has all been taken up and the final organization (of the group) took place in Montrose."

According to the *Montrose Press* of that city, the Montrose meeting moves the process forward as contracts are signed for the conduct of surveys related to what is now dubbed the "proposed Montrose interurban electric railway." Under a front-page headline "Railroad Talk," a speculative story attributed to the *Montrose Press* seems to hedge bets by declaring that "reports have persistently been circulated," but also that "no official connected with the road will verify the reports, neither have they been denied by anyone." What is known, the *Press* maintains, is that "Paret, the chief engineer of the road, has made another complete investigation of the proposed route, and that George W. Bruce of Delta, and Mr. Curtis of Cedaredge" have conferred with the road's directors and the chief engineer in regard to the route of the road in Delta County. The lack of more detailed and accurate information is attributed to "the reluctance of the railroad people to divulge their plans."

And yet Clyde Brewer, writing in the *Champion*, is optimistic that "enough is known to make it certain that Montrose and the (Surface Creek) valley are about to realize their dream of having an interurban road connect the various product centers with the markets. The officials of the road say that they will be ready to make a complete statement of progress within a very few days, and they promise the people of Montrose and the valley a pleasant surprise when they are ready to give out their plans."

Meanwhile, December is a busy month for the postal service. Sometime during the night, an unknown person picked the front door lock at the Eckert post office, entered the building, and stole $36.84 in cash, an 8-pound package of candy, and possibly other things. Postmaster Wenger distinctly recalls closing and securely locking the door only to find it ajar the next morning. So quietly did the robber work that the telephone central girl, who was asleep in the adjoining room, was not awakened. Since a money box containing more cash was overlooked, the whole affair is thought to be the work of a rank amateur. Still, there is no clue as to the perpetrator's identity.

A week later, an examination in connection with the Eckert post office robbery brings Post Office Inspector Williamson of Grand Junction to the Valley. Inspector Williamson also visits the Cedaredge post office where he finds everything to be satisfactory. The inspector praises the regularity with which the stage line handles the mails. He also predicts the likelihood that the Cedaredge operation will be promoted to a higher class—the postal receipts here justifying the change. Within days of the inspector's prediction, Postmaster Harry Cobbett receives what he views as "a very acceptable Christmas present" when a letter from the First Assistant Postmaster General confirms that the Cedaredge post office has been advanced from fourth to third class. The advancement means a step-up for postal service including the naming of the Cedaredge post office as an international money order office. The new designation also includes a tidy increase in the local postmaster's salary. It is uncertain what Cobbett's original rate of pay was, but, beginning January 1, 1911, his new compensation will be fixed at $1,100 per year.

Author's note: Under the provisions of an Act of Congress approved on March 3, 1883, the classification of post offices is to be primarily based on revenue, although population size is also considered. The details are a bit vague, but a third-class designation seems to have meant that a given post office was eligible for additional funding which could result in the hiring of carriers rather than relying exclusively on post office boxes or the handing out of mail during set hours at a central office location. It may also influence whether the advanced post office rents a space or has the latitude and funds to make other arrangements. A town classified second- and third-class could boast of the honor as an indication of civic progress. Moving up the postal food chain was good for business.

On a somber, yet critically necessary note, a communication from the Cemetery Association announces that December 12 has been set aside for removing the last of the bodies from the old cemetery. Under the banner "Another Removal Day," the message from C.S. Blanchard, association president, and Virgil Atchison, secretary, states: "This has been a big task, but one badly needing to be done in the interest of the public health and the men of the neighborhood have generously cooperated. Now it is requested that as many as can will turn out on next Monday and complete the work. Some will be needed at the new cemetery south of town and some at the old cemetery north of town. Come out, and if you can, bring pick and shovel."

In water news, fireworks at the annual meeting of the Surface Creek Ditch & Reservoir Company results, after a strong fight is made for certain candidates, in the election of Henry Hawker as president; John Griffith, secretary; and board members, H.W. Bull, T.J. Harshman, Roy A. Downs, J.O. Simpson, and W.A. Stark. The officers and board established, an assessment of $5 per share is "levied for the purpose of improvement, running expenses, and litigation over enlargement filings."

Apples are in the news as usual. Governor J.F. Shafroth issues an official call for the first annual convention of the American Apple Congress to be held in Denver in mid-December 1910. The call goes out to Colorado growers and also to other western apple growing states. The call acknowledges the rapid development of the apple industry in Colorado and her sister states. It also outlines an impressive array of issues to be addressed by the congress, ranging from fighting insect pests to systematizing the rules for grading and packing of apples. The *Champion* hopes that Cedaredge and the Surface Creek Valley will send a strong delegation to the pre-holiday congress. The Denver & Rio Grande Railway will offer special rates to those attending. Among others, F.W. Childs will probably act as a representative. Hopes are high that the congress will be a source of much benefit to the apple industry.

In other crop news, Valley residents are contemplating the impact of a rumor that the Grand Junction sugar beet factory may move its operation to Delta. The reason is that a large part of the beets which supply the factory are raised in Delta and Montrose Counties with the result that the crop must be hauled to Grand Junction for refining. Grand Junction is unhappy with the prospect, but, in the *Champion's* opinion, Delta is the logical point for the factory since it is centrally located in the growing region. Furthermore, because the Gunnison tunnel is ready for the business of supplying water, a vast amount of additional beet acreage will soon be opened up.

E.E. Bull arrives from his ranch southwest of town to share a list of premiums won at this autumn's National Horticultural Congress. Displayed at the congress site in Iowa, Mr. Bull's Champion apples won first and second prizes as did his Beach variety (also known as, the Apple of Commerce). His Black Ben Davis apples earned a first-place prize. Also honored were his Orange Quince and his Senator varieties which placed second and third. Most coveted was a special prize awarded to Mr. Bull for the best Black Ben Davis, which earned him possession of 250 one-year-old Black Ben trees for the planting.

Coverage of the Cedaredge Town Council meetings has become a regular feature. Present at December meetings are Mayor Smith and Trustees Rowbotham, Smethurst, James, Elhart, and Thompson. By council action, Mr. Henderson's petition to erect a frame residence on his lots is approved. In what seems like a highly appropriate move, a lumber bill is tabled. A sub-committee of trustees is appointed to confer with Mr. Phil Stephens, local civil engineer, who has established a baseline from which all future surveys in Cedaredge will hereafter be governed. Waterworks for Cedaredge are discussed with no definite action taken. A list of individual expenditures totaling $172.85 and $289.80 are enumerated and approved. R.V. Whinnery submits an application for a franchise for an electric light plant at Cedaredge. After lengthy discussion, the electric plant matter is tabled with a committee of five trustees appointed to investigate the proposal.

Without waiting on the committee report, the *Champion* forges ahead with a critique of the franchise application. The request for two years in which to have an electric light plant in operation is, the *Champion* feels, "an absurd thing to ask and expect to be granted. It would be a loop hole for all kinds of irregularities and would allow the petitioner the opportunity of holding a valuable privilege which he could later dispose of at a neat profit. If any profits of this kind are to be derived, the town should have them."

Another undesirable feature of the electric light plant petition is a request to grant to the franchise operators the use of Cedaredge's streets, alleys, and other public ways without giving the town anything in return. The newspaper is far from being opposed to an electric light plant at Cedaredge.

Public utilities are something every town wants and needs. But other towns have had sad experiences with outside investors.

In concluding his analysis, Publisher Brewer makes a series of elegant and insightful points. "The feeling at present," says the *Champion*, "seems very much in favor of a municipal water and light plant controlled and owned by the town. In light of this feeling, it would be well for the council, in the event a franchise is granted, to reserve a purchasing right after a certain period of years when the town is in better financial condition to shoulder the burden. With good prospects for a railroad in the near future, these matters will rapidly assume greater prominence and a little thought along these lines will probably be a big help in the future. Cedaredge is growing and will continue to grow, along with growth comes many of these problems in question which we must consider with a view to future generations not alone to our own good."

Mentions of motorized vehicles are beginning to appear in the *Champion* alongside advertisements for blacksmith services, harness-makers, and horses for sale. W.S. Grant adds a new employee, Hilbert Fogg, to his blacksmith shop. Arthur King is erecting a new building in Eckert with the intention of opening a blacksmith facility. I.C. Hall offers for sale a Maxwell Runabout—in fine condition with par-

The Elk Barn and AUTO LIVERY

Lovett & McGill, Proprietors

Stoddard-Dayton

——Our Fine Big——

Passenger Automobile

Is now at your service either **Day** or **Night**. By this means we can take you to Delta, Austin or other county points, quickly and comfortably. **Parties met anywhere by Appointment.**

Don't Forget That we can also give you a Firstclass Livery Team with or without drivers.

ticulars and price upon inquiry. Billy Eggleston and Dad Lambert are making regular trips to and from Delta each day using both the automobile and (horse-drawn) stage. They are prepared to carry passengers and anything customers may have to haul. Reachable using both phones, their Delta headquarters occupy the Osborne-Williams Drug Store.

Sam Lovett and his partner J.H. McGill seek to have things both ways by creating The Elk Barn and Auto Livery. Customers can be conveyed to Delta and elsewhere in a Stoddard-Dayton passenger automobile. Or they can elect the old-fashioned option and rent a buggy and livery team and be driven, or drive themselves, to their location.

Author's note: Helen Baker Austin's "Surface Creek Country" reports that Lovett, a member of the Elk's Lodge, had a large elk head painted on the front of The Elk Barn. According to Austin, the Stoddard-Dayton was red and was generally seen with its top down as shown in the advertisement on the preceding page. Describing the place as one might describe an urban bus station, Austin maintained that the Elk Barn was a spot "where transients could pass the time, or stretch out on the straw to sober up, if they had imbibed too freely." The partnership of Lovett and McGill was short-lived because H.P. Miller (who once operated the Bar I Ranch) and merchant W.F. Shinaman purchased the operation for a whopping $6,500. Helen Baker Austin's book is available for checkout at the Delta County Libraries.

In another indication that technology is sweeping into the Surface Creek Valley, the Crescent Amusement Company presents the luxury of a moving picture show at Austin, Eckert, and Cedaredge. The portable company moves up the Valley, entertaining Austin on Monday and Tuesday; Eckert on Wednesday and Thursday; and Cedaredge on Friday and Saturday. The exhibitors promise "a high-class Moving Picture Show. 3,000 feet of finest pictures obtainable, all clean, good subjects that will not hurt the feelings of the most refined taste; ladies and children especially invited. Come one and all. Admission is a dime each for either adult or child. The features are as follows: 1. "One Night and Then" (comedy drama), 2. "In Ancient Greece (dance in color), 3. "Cora, the Contraband's Daughter" (drama in color), 4. "Taming a Husband" (comedy drama), 5. "The Fence on Bar Z Ranch" (comedy), 6. "From Shadow to Sunshine" (a good story), and 7. "Mischievous Pet" (rip-roaring comedy).

Author's note: Actor, writer, producer, and director Gilbert M. Anderson (pictured here) was involved in hundreds of short films from 1907-1922. He played three rolls in the classic silent western "The Great Train Robbery" and is best remembered for his 148 short films in which he played the character Bronco Billy. He directed "The Fence on Bar Z Ranch" in 1910 and seventy other shorts—mostly thinly-plotted westerns. Comfortable in front and behind the camera, he received an honorary Oscar in 1958 as a motion picture pioneer. He died in 1971 at the age of 90.

So successful is their opening night in Cedaredge Hall, that the Crescent Amusement Company returns with a second full program of short moving pictures including: "The Mountain Lake, The Nightmare, Faithful, The Twisted Trail, The Banks of the Ganges, The Courting of the Merry Widow, The Milk Industry in the Alps, and The Tempestuous Adventures." The cost has risen to 20 cents for adults but remains a dime for children. Next on the program will be "Woman's Vanity, Punch and Judy, Sepoy's Wife, and The Golf Fiend."

In the realm of more physical pastimes than motion picture watching, a local football game takes place which creates considerable interest. The Cedaredge high school team plays against a team picked from around town. "The game," reports the *Champion*, "was strongly contested, each side having its own advantages. The high school was far ahead on team-work while the town team had the advantage of weight. When the smoke of battle cleared, it was found that neither side had scored." It is a result which fails to disappoint a good crowd of spectators who witnessed the contest. A re-match a few days later ends with the town team winning 5 to 0.

> *Author's note: Given the odd score of the Cedaredge re-match, one suspects the "football" played was soccer rather than American style football. Another explanation might be an error in scoring or the reporter's inability to grasp the scoring particulars.*

The Colorado Agricultural College at Fort Collins offers to train women for roles as wives, mothers, and housekeepers—that is to keep a proper home for their family. As the person who coordinates such training, Professor Mary F. Rausch declares: "Housekeepers must be trained. There will then be fewer divorces. Work becomes a joy and a pleasure when we have a special education for it. Housekeeping is a business, a profession, like any other business. More people engage in it than in any other occupation." As part of the curriculum, each female in Professor Rausch's department learns the care, training, and feeding of little children and each female is required to make a complete baby's outfit in order to earn her degree.

The Bank of Cedaredge has on hand an abundance of money for farm loans at reasonable rates and they urge readers to start "a check account" to broaden their business education and accumulate money.

Accidents continue to cloud the holiday season. While on her way home from Cedaredge, Mrs. G.A. Leinbach was thrown from her buggy, sustaining a broken collar bone. On the night of the accident—an evening of pitch darkness—the travelers were "trusting the team to follow the road, which they did not do and the buggy struck a large rock." Although the bone was broken in two places, Mrs. Leinbach is rapidly recovering. Mr. Goin of Eckert was seriously hurt by the breaking of a binding chain which failed to secure a load of pipe.

Without citing the source, the *Champion* devotes a full fifth of a column to a Colorado cheer:

> Call: "Where's the land of sunshine?"
> Response: *"COLORADO!"*
> What's the center of the universe?
> *COLORADO!*
> What's the best place to live in?
> *COLORADO!*
> Where?
> *COLORADO!*
> Where?
> *COLORADO!*
> Where?
> *COLORADO!*
> Spell heaven—
> *C-O-L-O-R-A-D-O!*
> Potatoes! Where?
> *COLORADO!*
> Apples! Where?
> *COLORADO!*

A scheme to dam the North Fork of the Gunnison River below Hotchkiss is uncovered. The bogus plan of storing water to irrigate land south of Delta ends in the arrest of seven officers of the Riverside Colonization Company—an enterprise which operated chiefly out of Denver and Grand Junction. Locals and some government officials had felt from the start that the idea was ridiculous. The schemers had much less land and water than advertised and the entire project was proven a fake. Investors who put money into the project have lost all hope of recovery.

The States Coal Mine has returned to its old entry point to alleviate customers having to make a "hard pull" to reach the scales. According to C.D. Daniels, mine manager, the enterprise can supply any amount of nice clean coal.

R.P. James is the man to see for those who wish to join the Western Slope Poultry and Pet Stock Association. A one-dollar bill will secure membership. A new proprietor has purchased the fixtures and butcher business of Buzzard Brothers. The new owner is W.N. Parker and he expects to add to his stock and equipment as rapidly as business demands.

Construction is booming. Otto C. Peterson is building a 6-room residence on his Cactus Park ranch. Jacob Kangas is erecting a small residence on a plot of ground purchased from H.B. Cook. A. Bacon sells his Cedaredge residence to Mrs. Buzzard and moves to the Mountjoy residence east of town. John and Sam Christman purchase three lots in the Kennedy & Duffield addition and will start work at once on a residence. W.S. Pickett erects a small residence on South Main Street. Nat Thomas sells his interest in the Grand Mesa sawmill to Jas. Trian. Mr. Thomas will now turn his attention to the clearing of 100 acres for Dr. Whiting. Harry Stewart has the foundation completed for erection of yet another bungalow in the land addition which bears his name. R.P. James has the Stewart contract. In other real estate news, E.D. Smith of the Cedaredge Realty Company returns from a trip to the other side of the Rockies to report that "prospects for an influx of settlers" are "very good as many people in the east are now looking toward the western slope for homes."

A newspaper feature entitled "Deals in Dirt" delineates a steadily growing wave of real estate deals and transfers. Of particular interest are multi-acre tracts of the Bar-I Ranch sold to individual parties as well as sections of purchased land being set to orchards and three lots which are purchased by the Baptist church.

The tax levy, as fixed by the board of (county) commissioners, makes an assessment of 57 mills on Cedaredge property which is the lowest assessment of any town in the county.

Technology continues to make news. R.V. Whinnery of Read is a visitor investigating the matter of installing an electric lighting plant at Cedaredge. He's not yet prepared to make a report on the matter, though the *Champion* feels the proposition looks good at first glance. The Co-operative telephone scene is improved with a new line added between Cedaredge and Austin. The Colorado Telephone Company employs a force of men to string cable in preparation for the relocation of their Central office to the Bolton & Smith Building.

Author's note: The town of Read, Colorado, which used to be the center of a burgeoning sugar beet industry, is essentially gone. The Delta-Montrose Electric Association (DMEA) maintains a branch office in the vicinity of the vanished town which has mostly reverted to an industrial park and farmland. The old site lies southeast of the intersection of Colorado State Highways 65 and 92.

The Valley's winter climate has been rainy, the wet weather resulting in muddy roads. But the challenging climate doesn't dampen the spirits of the Baptist congregation. Despite the cold, eighty young folks show up for Sunday school. Youngsters and adults celebrate the welcome news that the church is installing a new furnace—a standard hot air heating plant. Holiday sermon topics include "An Old-Fashioned Sermon" and "Edison and the Golden Rule." Dr. Stephenson will give his popular lecture, "A Trip to the Tropics," at the Baptist Church under the auspices of the Ladies' Auxiliary. The Sunday school is to have a library. Books in good condition are needed. They need not be religious books. Good fiction, history, and children's books are all needed. The Sunday school will catalogue the books, cover them with dust jackets, and appoint a librarian. The congregation, as well as many parties outside the church, will donate books. Donations are expected from other parts of Colorado and from distant states. The call for books yields an initial total of 50 donated volumes.

In other church news, the men's chorus of the Methodist Episcopal Church will sing at both holiday services. In addition to services at the Cedaredge location, the pastor will preach at the Cedar Mesa schoolhouse. Holiday sermons include a series which stresses sins which Jesus frequently denounced and an attempt will be made to show their relation to life today.

The series begins with "Hypocrisy" and will later touch on "Covetousness" and "Retribution." On Christmas Day and evening, there is special music and the Sunday school students perform a cantata. The ladies of the Methodist church hold a holiday fair at Cedaredge Hall featuring fancy articles which make nice Christmas presents. Offerings include aprons, a beautiful silk quilt, and assorted cotton comforters. Refreshments are provided. The fair nets $80. Ever active, the ladies also serve dinner to men working on the new parsonage.

Frank H. Wilson and Jas. Walsh have occasion to journey to Delta to attend the Catholic Fair given by the Ladies Aid group of that church. They enjoy the event and Mr. Wilson wins a door prize. Following similar meetings in Paonia and Delta, Cedaredge hosts a mass meeting to promote the idea of organizing a local branch of a Delta County Young Men's Christian Association. Traveling Y.M.C.A. libraries are established in Cedaredge and Crawford. A physician in Delta offers to teach first aid to a class of boys and the U.S. Department of Agriculture will work with the county in extending agricultural education to boys. Delta and Cedaredge Y.M.C.A. supporters organize Bible study groups. The Cedaredge group has 15 participants.

Classified advertisements include a note from Brown's Confectionary that his book exchange is running "full blast." Flapjack mix is available at Blanchard & Stockham as well as a fine assortment of Christmas candies, nuts, dates, and figs. At the Cedaredge Meat Market, T.J. Roberts makes two important announcements: dill pickles have arrived and a barrel of fine sauerkraut has just been opened. In an announcement which is lost in translation, the Cedaredge Hardware Company declares: "We will give piano certificates on your account, new or old, between now and January 15th." The hardware company also offers special holiday prices on top-notch buggies.

W.E. Steele is offering a reward for a lady's gold watch lost at or near Eckert. Allan King, proprietor of the Cedaredge Feed Store, will pay market prices for customer produce and his shop located south of Cedaredge Hall carries an assortment of hay, grain, and feed. Fred Wettrich has, at his ranch 2½ miles west of Cedaredge, "a thorobred Duroc boar and full-blood Jersey bull. Service fee for the former $1, for the latter $2."

*Author's note: Mr. Wettrich's classified advertisement does not contain a spelling error. The use of the term **thorobred** to describe a pure-bred animal—as opposed to the modern spelling as **thoroughbred**—was widespread in the 1900's up to and including the roaring twenties when language, hemlines, and music shifted into cultural overdrive. The old spelling employed in Wettrich's ad seemed to fall out of vogue only to reappear in modern times as a nostalgic artifice, along the lines of naming an antique store "Ye Olde Shoppe." There are other instances of passe terms popping up in the pages of the* Champion *such as the use of the term "milch cow" which, as stated earlier, is another way of saying "milk cow."*

Mrs. J.E. Harral, who serves as agent for the Denver Music Company, posts an "Important" suggestion to "make a wise expenditure of your Xmas money. Buy a piano for educating your children and the pleasure of your whole family. Come and see a fine piano and get prices." Mrs. Harral lists her address as "Cedarforty," ¼ mile east of Cedaredge.

Author's note: Encouraged by extension agents and other advisers, farmers and ranchers have taken to naming their spreads and even acquiring stationary and envelopes so as to represent their farm or ranch as a business.

Christmas postal cards, letters, and fancy cards are on sale at Brown's Confectionery. Eastman Kodak cameras and needed supplies for processing film and prints in a home darkroom can be purchased at Davis Drug Company with prices ranging from one dollar to $25. A seasonal sack of Mistletoe Flour as well as men's, boy's, and children's shoes can be had at Barrere's store. Lewis, the Jeweler, is offering a line of Christmas stock.

Not content to serve as merely a seller of furniture, rugs, and ranges, an enterprising entrepreneur asks readers, "Are you satisfied with the undertaking service you are getting? If not, call H.K. Correll, day or night. I ask but one profit. Can get to Cedaredge as quick as anybody from Delta."

Frank Wescott, the popular Cedaredge photographer, asks readers, "What's more appropriate than a photo for Xmas taken in your own home which gives a natural expression especially to the little one?"

Somewhere between Eckert and Cedaredge, a baby's long white coat has gone missing. The finder is urged to return same to the *Champion* office or the Eckert Store. D.W. Stemple, located on the lower end of Cedar Mesa, offers the following goods in a pre-holiday private sale: two good mares (weight 1,300); two milch cows; one hog; two bee stands; a good wagon; harness and other farming utensils; about 35 tons of hay; one 12 x 16 tent; 60 quarts of fruit; household goods; a dresser of drawers; a bedstead; and a sanitary couch.

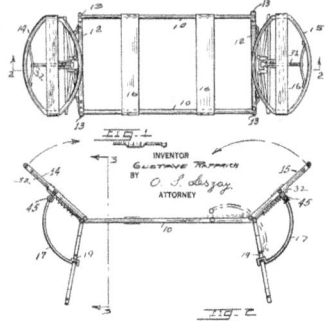

Holiday shopping inducements continue to tempt buyers. The operators of B. Barrere & Company—who have recently bought the J.K. Grant store—announce a sale designed to expire just after Christmas. Shoes, coats, gloves, overalls, pants, underwear, and sweaters—all winter needs at greatly reduced "prices which have never been given before."

Sherd's will be hosting Santa Claus. How does Sherd's know Santa is coming? The store reports receiving a telegram to that effect. Not only will the store serve as Santa's southern headquarters, the enterprising shop has also established a competition to select the most popular married lady on Surface Creek. Readers are invited to vote for themselves or a friend. Each cash purchase of 25 cents earns the privilege of casting 25 votes for the woman of one's choice. The winner will receive a set of hand-painted cups and saucers. The contest generates such a flood of interest that no fewer than 34 married women are nominated. Mrs. Lizzie Bowness of Austin prevails with 1,350 votes, followed by Mrs. Lusi Ladvala with 850, Mrs. Will Lovell—550, Mrs. Kate Lovett—475, Mrs. Ed January—375, and Mrs. Etta Parker—also 375. Several others finish out of the money.

The Bank of Cedaredge is distributing calendars featuring an impressive image of a painting by Thomas Moran entitled "A Summer Squall."

In a repeat of last year's holiday contest, Brown's Confectionery invites shoppers to "Follow the Rainbow" and guess how much cash is displayed in their "Pot of Money." Brown's also offers a holiday count-down in their display ads notifying the buying public how many shopping days remain until Christmas. Davis Drug Company (aka Cedaredge Drug) is also repeating a previous contest by giving away a beautiful doll and sweetening the prize with a chocolate set and hand-painted after-dinner plates. One chance given with each 25-cent purchase. No word on who won the plates, but the chocolate set was won by R.P. James and E.F. Boles claimed the doll.

The Cedaredge Hardware Company offers a few Christmas gift suggestions: silver knives and forks, table and tea spoons, nickel tea and coffee pots, embroidery and dressmaking scissors, pocket knives, safety razors, a new range, a new sewing machine, and nickel-plated and fancy parlor lamps. A new policy of renting sewing machines is announced by the hardware company.

As an appreciation of cash customers, Shinaman's Cash Bazaar will supply shoppers with one high grade silver-plated teaspoon with every dollar purchase. "Let your dollars work," they suggest. Shinaman's advertises their store as "Holiday Headquarters" for toys, games, and knick-knacks for the children as well as a "selected line of novel and useful articles for the whole family. All Goods plainly price-marked." After the Christmas selling season passes, the large emporium of Blanchard & Stockham will be operated upon a strictly cash basis. Cash is also preferred by J.K. Grant who, in a not-so-gentle notice, reminds those who owe debts to his recently-closed store that overdue accounts are waiting at the Bank of Cedaredge to be paid.

Author's note: 1910 fell squarely in the middle of a mild, but lingering economic downturn. Prices were falling and consumers were tempted to purchase, on credit, goods which might be considered luxuries. Cash was scarce and competition for buyers was keen. When unpaid accounts mounted, using the bank to collect debts was a merchant's last resort. Eventually, as the economy fluctuated, Shinaman, Grant, Blanchard & Stockham, and other Surface Creek Valley traders elected to do business on a strictly cash basis. Before he left the merchant life to concentrate on ranching, Grant followed Shinaman's lead by re-branding his general emporium Grant's Cash Store.

In a holiday inducement which seems familiar, the *Champion* announces an opportunity it identifies as "Big Bargains in Periodicals and Newspapers for 1911." Here are the details as summarized in a full-page advertisement: "The *Champion* has made arrangements with one of the largest Magazine and Newspaper agencies in the United States by which we can give you the choice of more than 1,000 Newspapers and Magazines published in the United States at a greatly reduced price. We also give you the benefit of our commissions by offering the *Surface Creek Champion,* (your home paper) at only $1.50 when taken in connection with any two magazines mentioned in our list which will be mailed upon request."

To show that the newspaper means what it says, four combinations (or "clubs") are outlined in the advertisement including this one:

Ladies Home Journal:	$1.50
Saturday Evening Post:	1.50
Surface Creek Champion:	2.00
Total:	5.00
Our Price:	4.50
Savings to you:	.50

Author's note: This strategy was apparently a new approach to increasing subscriptions, not only for small local newspapers, but for nationally distributed publications. One clue that more than one newspaper was trumpeting this offer is that the Champion *erred in not inserting their newspaper name in the proper space to override the phrase (your home paper.) Despite this oversight, a full-page ad of this sort with gigantic headlines would have been difficult to ignore. The lower portion of the page, just above "SURFACE CREEK CHAMPION, Cedaredge, Colorado," clarifies that the "clubs" shown are merely examples of what can be found in a big catalog which provides a full list of magazine/newspaper bargains. If all this sounds familiar, it may be because the concept seems to foreshadow today's Publishers Clearing House promotions—minus the fabulous cash sweepstakes administered by PCH. Admittedly, it's not a direct link because PCH didn't exist until 1953 when east-coast entrepreneur Harold Metz was working out of his basement to sell magazine subscriptions door-to-door. He thought up the sweepstakes in 1967 to boost subscriptions and the rest, as they say, is history. Most of the magazines listed in the* Champion *advertisement are unrecognizable to modern audiences. The foregoing example includes the most familiar, although the* Ladies Home Journal—*which launched in 1883—ceased publication in 2016. Some of the other publications in the December 1911 promotion may ring a bell. They included:* Success Magazine *(a business magazine which is still published);* Cosmopolitan *and* Woman's Home Companion; McClure Magazine *and* Everybody's Magazine *(muck-raking (i.e., investigative journalism) publications which also served as platforms for well-known fiction writers), and* Delineator *(a woman's magazine which included sewing patterns).*

Cedaredge's postmaster begins "a crusade against smoking in the post office during the time when the evening mail is being distributed. Considerable complaint has been made by ladies who wait for mail that the smoke was very offensive. Signs have been posted in conspicuous places and by this method the postmaster hopes to abate the nuisance."

To assist readers in accomplishing holiday travel, the Denver & Rio Grande Railroad is offering special low fares to and from all points in Colorado and New Mexico. Passengers must return by January 3, 1911. Of particular interest to long-distance travelers may be the railway's electric-lighted sleeping cars. Particulars may be had by calling the Rio Grande Agent. As an additional promotion, the Railroad is sending out Christmas cards this year. In other railroad news, owing to a change in the time of arrival of the morning train at Delta, the Cedaredge post office is informed that the stage need not leave Cedaredge until one hour later than at present. This adjustment will make the leaving time, on the Cedaredge end, eight o'clock in the morning rather than seven. Inasmuch as the regular stage carries not only passengers, but also regular cargos of mail to and from Delta, the time change will give citizens more time to post their outgoing packages and correspondence. Mail can now be received as late as 7:45 a.m. but not later. This will make things more convenient for both the postmaster and the stage driver, especially during the winter months.

A new business which opens for Christmas shopping is The Variety Store. Operated by O.W. Overhults, whose brother is an assistant cashier at the bank, the store is situated in the east room of the Rogers building. The 1910 supply chain frustrates the new merchant and he's a bit frazzled because the bulk of his goods fail to arrive. When his doors open at 10 o'clock on Christmas Eve day, Overhults does not have much on hand to tempt the last-minute holiday shopper. His disappointing opening day is somewhat over-ridden by news that, commencing in January, he will be handling all incoming and outgoing express mail, packages, and other matter for the stage line.

Reports from Tongue Creek indicate that Hiram Burritt will go to Delta for a nasal operation. Miss Sterlie Wallace and Clyde Reed are married in a pre-holiday wedding at the home of the groom's parents. Dr. J.E. McConnell has the misfortune, while chopping beets, of also severing the tips of three fingers off his left hand. Glen Adams, a young man who has been a cripple all his life and who was recently ailing, is discovered dead in bed. The deceased is the brother of Mrs. Will Hawkins.

On Cedar Mesa, work on the Lone Pine ditch is stopped due to lack of funds, but a meeting of the stockholders produces an appropriation and work resumes. A son is born to Mr. and Mrs. William Busey. Miss Nellie Trickel becomes the bride of Earle Frost with Reverend Hill of Eckert officiating. Four horses are missing, lost or strayed, from Clarence A. Smith's Cedar Mesa ranch. Two colts and two fillies are described in detail and all are bearing the brand of a "lazy three" (a three rotated sideway to rest on its back) with the letter "H" underneath. A reward of five dollars is offered for the animals' return.

In Eckert, Guy Barnes opens a barber shop in the settlement's pool hall. W.T. Smith and daughter Alice are confined to their homes with typhoid fever. Mrs. Maud Lamar is compelled by the death of her mother, Mrs. Mary Griffith, to travel to Lake City. She is joined in her grief by the decedent's sister Mrs. Watts and the dearly departed's nieces Mrs. Lizzie Bowness and Mrs. J.W. Taylor, all of whom travel to Lake City. Having reached the age of 62 years, Mrs. Griffith died of pneumonia. Eckert resident, Miss Verna Kehmier, is united in marriage to Mr. Walter Johnson. The young couple is preparing to move to Texas. Dr. Ira J. Clark has moved to Eckert where he will begin building up a practice. H.K. Ferguson returns from attending the Apple Congress in Denver. The Eckert Store is remodeled and new show cases added. Several residents are ill with the "gripp."

Author's note: Often misspelled as "gripp," the grippe (or, to use the French name, la grippe) was once a common term for infectious influenza. Cases were on the rise in 1910, however medical professionals and demographic statisticians were beginning to suspect that many cases attributed to influenza or the grippe were misdiagnosed by doctors and coroners using what had become a convenient, catchall term. Essentially respiratory in nature, the grippe manifested symptoms not unlike the modern pandemic of COVID-19 and its variants, including difficulty breathing, fatigue, high fever, and loss of the senses of taste and smell.

In society and club news, at the invitation of Phil K. Stephens, those interested in forming a Knights of Pythias Lodge are requested to assemble at the Stewart Realty Company. Both old members and prospective members are urged to attend. The cost to attend the Christmas dance at Eckert Hall is one dollar (supper extra) and a large and jolly crowd takes advantage of the opportunity. The Ladies Aid Fair serves refreshments, including oyster stew.

Modern Woodmen officers are chosen to be O.J. McReynolds, J.S. Wright, J.C. Rowbotham, Roy A. Downs, H.E. Rowbotham, and O.E.

Taylor each will assume a unique role in the organization. At this same meeting, eight new men were elected to membership with their initiation to be conducted by a team from Delta after the first of the year.

Formed last month in November, "The Cedaredge Woman's Literary Club" meets at the home of Mrs. Roy A. Downs to continue the new club's momentum. Officers elected are: Mrs. H.P. Johnson, president; Mrs. Nellie Mills, first vice-president; Mrs. Lola Bull, second vice-president; Mrs. Helen Buol, treasurer; and Mrs. Norine Overhults, secretary. The club consists of the following charter members: Mesdames H.P. Johnson, Lizzie Bolton, Nellie Mills, Myrtle Downs, Helen Buol, Mamie Hocker, Etta Curtis, Emily Sherd, Lola Bull, W.W. Dingman, May Atchison, and Norine Overhults.

Mrs. C.S. Blanchard has returned from Denver where she underwent a medical operation and she is pleased to be home for Christmas. Mr. Blanchard is jubilant over the prospects for his wife's complete recovery.

Holiday babies arrive. Mr. and Mrs. Finley Roberts welcome a daughter and Mr. and Mrs. J.F. Foster celebrate a son. Mr. and Mrs. Guy Atkinson rejoice over the amazing birth of a 10-pound baby boy.

The *Champion's* Cedar Mesa correspondent is cautiously optimistic to report that Mrs. Benson and other residents are slowly improving and that no new cases of typhoid are reported. Cedar Mesa's own W.G. Davidson returns from a trip to Glenwood Springs and Grand Junction in time to assist with the work of installing the new heating plant in the Cedaredge Baptist Church. Repairs on the Lone Pine Ditch are completed and the water turned in which is a great relief to many living along the ditch who were greatly inconvenienced by the lack of water. Mr. Gorsuch hauls four big loads of wheat to Austin for shipment. A holiday dance at the Boscobel Orchards house will be chaperoned by Mr. and Mrs. Webb of Payne's Mesa. Before the school closed for the holidays, the students were surprised with a treat of candy, popcorn, and peanuts.

On the "Young People" page, a tongue-twister poses the question: "Why did Doctor Foster go to Glouchester in a shower of rain? And step in a puddle up to the middle, when he could have gone there by train?"

Notes from the Rural Free Delivery carrier include an announcement that a number of new boxes have been put up. These include: Will Lowell on the Otto Peterson place; Wm. Caldwell on the Koch place; Leinbach on Morris' corner; E.J. Ward and Mr. Utterback on Flint's corner; J.K. Grant and A.B. Stetson on Plimpton's corner; Mrs. Susan Brown on Ben Reed's corner; and B.F. Ross on his east corner. There are now 109 families on the route, not counting those away for the winter. Mr. Gridley has built a good barn. G.E. Morris is excavating for a new house and Ben Reed is nearly finished with his substantial house situated on his corner. Wm. Metzger's new residence is also almost finished. The roadman, Henry Stolte, and nearby residents are doing a good job of maintaining the road between McKinnon's and Jacoby's corners.

In making his appointed rounds, the carrier voices a concern that a number on the route do not seem to understand the use of the signal flag on the boxes. He gives detailed instructions on the use of the flag and requests that patrons clip his article and paste it up where it can be seen and remembered. During a recent visit from the postal inspector, the RFD carrier was glad to report that patrons appreciate the rural route very highly. If routes are to be cut, this one will not be among those to be dropped.

The inspector emphasized that RFD patrons must erect proper rural route boxes and postmaster D.C. Townsend has laid out the particulars. There are four criteria. First, the box must be located where it is easy to drive up to and drive away from and rocks or other obstructions must be cleared out. Second, the post box must be large enough and set deep enough to be strong and substantial. Third, the box must be facing the road so the carrier can see into it easily. Fourth, at a point not less than five feet from the ground, with five and one-half feet being better, the box must be placed at the end of an arm of not less than between eighteen inches and two feet long. This height is vital so that the carrier's buggy can easily drive under the box to serve it. The arm itself must be well-braced in a solid manner. Two good braces on either side of the post are ideal.

In response to these regulations, E.W. Stolte makes a steel brace of a spring tooth from a harrow, bolting one end to the post and the other to the box which makes a fine method. J.O. Caldwell and E.R. Humphrey have boxes which need some adjustments. G.A. Leinbach and G.H. Webb are touted as having an excellent model of an erected box. Anyone wishing to see a diagram of how a box should be erected can call at the post office or travel out and take a look at Mr. Webb's box. The carrier has authority to report ill-made boxes, but has no desire to do so. RFD patrons are asked to attend to their boxes.

A new U.S. post office order indicates that first class mail bearing a return address will, if undeliverable, be sent back to the sender five days after its arrival. Under the former rule, this class of mail was held for 30 days before being returned. This change will do away with considerable delay and will relieve postmasters and clerks of the necessity of handling accumulated undelivered mail.

A vintage photograph adds pictorial weight to a solution which the *Champion* has been advocating since 1908. Portraying the Western Slope State Normal Building, the photo shows the $50,000 structure erected in Gunnison by the State of Colorado. The *Champion* has long advocated that Western Slope communities support the Gunnison site as the most logical location for an institution of higher learning on this side of the Rocky Mountains. Even with support from the *Champion* and others, the fight to secure a college in Western Colorado has raged for more than 20 years. Built of red brick and native stone and situated on an ideal site overlooking the town of Gunnison, the building seems, at last, to lay to rest the wrangling which delayed its construction.

Christmas weddings continue as Miss Edith Bowness and Mr. Geo. Trickel exchange vows at the bride's home. In attendance, in addition to the bride's mother, are Miss Amelia Pelazini and Mr. David Jones. Mr. Trickel expects to secure employment with the U.S. Forest Service which will govern where the couple will locate in the future. Miss Ida Closson becomes the bride of Mr. Frank Hamilton. Clyde Reed is best man and Miss Matilda Pelazini of Eckert serves as bridal maid. Miss Emma Welty played the wedding march. Miss Edith Walls, a former teacher at the Trickle School, is wed to Mr. Oliver Barnes. United in matrimony are Tom Griffith and Miss Sarah Coffee of Austin.

Final Thoughts on Christmases 1904 to 1910

As author and reader, we have taken a journey through time, following the evolution of the Surface Creek Valley from a loose affiliation of farmers, ranchers, merchants, orchard cultivators, artisans, and laborers to an array of incorporated towns which are sailing into unchartered waters as they grapple with the challenges of roads, sidewalks, transportation, water, and power while also dreaming of a boundless future. Along the way we've encountered a pious people, proud of their churches, resolute in educating their children, visiting and uplifting neighbors, reveling in community entertainments, rejoicing in births and marriages, mourning and honoring their dead, harnessing land and water, grumbling about the weather, but also celebrating the seasons as they relish the bounty of their verdant valley and bask in the majestic glory of Grand Mesa.

Our guide has been Clyde W. Brewer and his blossoming *Surface Creek Champion* which, true to its name, has relentlessly championed and boosted the town, the Valley, and the Western Slope. An obvious idealist but also pragmatically honest, Brewer has faithfully chronicled the steady rise of a town's identity, a Valley's personality, and a Western Slope's legacy.

In the final days of 1910, it seems fitting that the *Champion's* sister newspaper—a periodic ally and sometime rival—the nearby *Delta Independent* should pen a eulogy to its northern neighbor. The *Independent's* glowing report may be the best account we have of how the Valley was viewed by an unbiased observer who was on the outside, looking in. On the following page, in its entirety, is the *Independent's* December 23, 1910, tribute to the Surface Creek Valley:

Good Words for this Valley

No prettier, more healthy or better farming and fruit growing section lies out of doors than the Surface Creek section.

Splendidly watered by numerous creeks and canals, fed from scores of big lakes on Grand mesa, and with soils peculiarly adapted for its various crops, Surface Creek will stand for all time as a banner district.

It is claimed that but one fruit failure has occurred in this district from late frosts in its history of apple and peach growing of eighteen years.

It is sheltered by Grand mesa mountain, towering to a height of ten thousand feet on the north, and on whose flat top are situated the score of big lakes which give it an unfailing supply of water for irrigation and domestic purposes. Here also are situated some of the largest and most valuable coal deposits to be found in the United States

The record of Surface Creek fruits has been their productiveness and high quality, and the same can be said of all other products.

The valley is peopled with a splendid class of citizen land owners, who are all substantial, and many of them have grown wealthy from the products of the soil.

The following brief statements tell much, and supply in concise form, valuable information regarding the Surface Creek portion of Delta county.

The great fruit section commences some six miles from Delta and is five miles in width by seventeen miles in length, varying in altitude from 5,100 to 6,500 feet. It has within its borders fourteen schools, six post offices, three churches, telephones and rural mail delivery. In fact, all the conveniences of suburban country.

Though limited in acreage, the valley has some two hundred lakes on the summit of this flat-topped mountain, supplying a water system sufficient for double the acreage of the valley.

Cedaredge, the largest town in the Surface Creek valley, lies ten miles from the shipping point of Austin, on the broad gauge of the Denver & Rio Grande Railroad. This little city is incorporated, has several churches, a high school, bank, newspaper and some twenty business places. Eckert lies midway between Cedaredge and Austin and is the heart of the valley. A store, one church and four business houses comprise this little village.

Austin and Cory, thriving orchard sections of the valley, have two and one-half miles of solid orchard and are situated on the railroad.

At Austin are packing houses and a canning factory, stores and a bank recently founded. —*Delta Independent*

The Surface Creek Valley Historical Society
and the *Champion* Newspaper

History buffs can thank the Surface Creek Valley Historical Society (SCVHS) for accomplishing the ambitious goal of making past issues of the *Surface Creek Champion* accessible to the public. As a result of their foresight and planning, some 12,000 pages of the historic newspaper have been converted to digital media, which makes every issue of the vintage newspaper viewable and searchable.

The Historical Society has also preserved another vestige of the newspaper's bygone era. The *Champion's* original paper cutter is on display at Pioneer Town, a historic village owned and operated by the Society.

Surviving relatives of Clyde W. Brewer and his wife Alpha, still reside in the Surface Creek Valley. In 2019, as part of its commitment to resurrect the *Champion*, the Historical Society presented their Pioneer Award to Mr. and Mrs. Brewer and their descendants, several of whom were in attendance to accept the honor.

Donate to SCVHS and join the Society!

The Surface Creek Valley Historical Society (SCVHS) welcomes donations to support their work of preserving and honoring local history. The non-profit society operates Pioneer Town, an historic village which features vintage buildings and exhibits. The society also sponsors special events throughout the year and the group welcomes volunteers and new members.

To join the Society, visit the SCVHS website: pioneertown.org. Contributions may be made to the "Surface Creek Valley Historical Society" and mailed to P.O. Box 906, Cedaredge, CO 81413. For further information call 970-856-7554 or email scvhistsoc@gmail.com.

The Colorado Historic Newspapers Collection

As a service of the Colorado State Library, the *Surface Creek Champion*—along with over 600 other Colorado newspapers—can now be accessed without charge through the website coloradohistoricnewspapers.org. The following information appears on their website:

"A service of the Colorado State Library, the Colorado Historic Newspapers Collection (CHNC) currently includes more than 2.5 million digitized pages, representing more than 620 individual newspaper titles published in Colorado from 1859 up thru 2021. Due to copyright restrictions, the CHNC does not always include newspapers published after 1926, but the CHNC can digitize beyond 1926 if publisher permission can be secured. And, best of all, the CHNC can be browsed and searched for free! Ongoing support for maintaining and providing access to the CHNC is paid for with federal and state funds administered by the Colorado State Library. We continue to add new pages to the CHNC when community funding is secured to pay the costs of digitization."

The CHNC also accepts donations from users who visit their website.

Brewer Family Ties

More than a dozen descendants of Clyde W. and Alpha Brewer were on hand in February 2019 to accept a Pioneer Award presented by the Surface Creek Valley Historical Society. Mr. Brewer was the primary publisher of the *Surface Creek Champion* newspaper which served the Valley from 1904–1943.

Left to right, back row: Bob Brewer, Geoff Kunkel, Cindy Kruger, Yvonne Simmons, Bruce Bertram, Donna (Ankenbauer) Bryson, Sheri McFadden, Mike Bryson. Front, left to right: Kathie Johnson, Susan Kunkel, Myrna Bertram, Don McFadden. Seated: Carolynn Andersen.
(Photo by Don Benjamin)

Other Resources

The Delta County Libraries collection includes books about the Surface Creek Valley. Those with an (*) are also available at the Pioneer Town Gift Shop in Cedaredge. Interested readers are encouraged to review these publications:

- *Surface Creek Country: By a Native Daughter*—Hazel Baker Austin
- *Once Upon Surface Creek*—Doyle Kline
- *Blue Shaded Mountains* and other poems—Phil Ellsworth (available online only at: https://www.poems.philellsworth.com/)
- **A History of the Surface Creek Valley & the Town of Cedaredge*—Ronn Brewer
- **Life on the Creek: Personal Recollections of a Childhood on Surface Creek in Western Colorado*—Evelyn Grow Helm and Sybil Grow Moschetti
- **Following the Sandhill Cranes in Colorado* and other books—Evelyn Horn
- **The Awesome 'Dobie Badlands* and *Island in the Sky: The Story of Grand Mesa* and other books—Muriel Marshall

❦ Index ❧

Rhoades—23
Richardson—29
Riley—9
Rist—23, 58
Ritter—3
Roberts—91, 99
Ross—100
Rowbotham—20, 34, 66, 71, 72, 84, 98
Rowell—54, 66
Runnoe—65
Ryan—67
Sanford—12, 51
Schoenter—23
Scott—44
Seaton—43
Shackleford—35
Shafroth—59, 83
Shelledy—37, 75
Sherd—33, 38, 48, 69, 93, 99
Shinaman—29, 68, 86, 94, 95
Shurd—17
Simmons—58, 105
Simpson—53, 74, 83
Sisk—9
Skinner—9, 11, 29, 30, 59, 60
Smethurst—84
Smith—3, 22, 70, 84, 89, 90, 97, 98
Sprague—80

Springer—47
Stanford—70
Stark—83
States—64, 73, 89
Steele—2, 18, 91
Stell—48, 58, 62
Stemple—93
Stephens—48, 70, 80, 84, 98
Stephenson—90
Stetson—100
Stevens—35
Stewart—89, 98
Stockham—7, 11, 25, 33, 50, 69, 70, 91, 94
Stolte—7, 36, 100
Stone—51
Stowe—3
Sturdevant—43, 66
Taft—21, 52
Taylor—30, 98, 99
Teachout—12
Thomas—62, 89
Thompson—27, 84
Tim—4, 24
Townsend—100
Trian—89
Trickel—4, 78, 97, 101
Trickle—3, 4, 11, 21
Turner—47
Utterback—47, 100
Van Aken—9, 31
Vanaken—45, 52

Walker—45
Wallace—97
Walls—101
Walsh—66, 91
Ward—100
Warhing—45
Watts—98
Webb—7, 18, 22, 33, 45, 62, 99, 100
Weir—8
Welch—66
Welty—101
Wenger—10, 81
Wescott—92
Westen—49
Wettrich—91, 92
Whinnery—84, 90
White—38, 45, 58, 70
Whiting—37, 89
Williamson—62, 82
Wilson—34, 91
Winters—66
Wood—2
Woodward—9, 21, 39, 65, 68
Wright—45, 68, 98
Yeoman—73
Young—74
Zaninetti—9, 12, 25, 67
Zanola—2
Zeigler—18

Names of Businesses and Places:

Alabama Nursery Company—38
Aspen Democrat—60
Bank of Cedaredge—34, 49, 51, 72, 87, 94
Bar-I Ranch—89
Barrere & Company/Store—92, 93
Blanchard & Stockham—11, 25, 33, 50, 69, 91, 94
Bolton & Smith Building—90
Boscobel Orchards—99
Brown's Confectionary—68, 70, 91, 92, 94

Brown Palace Hotel—59
Bull Ranch—47
Burritt Ranch—67
Butt & Finch Ranch/Place—20
Buzzard Brothers—89
Buzzard & Sons—19
Cedar Mesa Ditch & Reservoir Company—75
Cedaredge Pool/Billiard Hall—5, 72
Cedaredge Confectionery—17, 18

Names of Churches, Schools, and Organizations:

About the Author

Donald Paul Benjamin is an award-winning novelist. Born in Greeley, a mid-sized settlement on Colorado's eastern plains, he grew up writing stories about local characters and sketching animals on his family's small acreage. As a teen, he worked on his high school newspaper. Upon graduation in 1963, he enlisted in the U.S. Army, serving three years as a military journalist, including a tour in Korea. Honorably discharged, he earned his teaching degree from the University of Northern Colorado (UNC). He taught first grade, then served as UNC's first campus ombudsman. In 1982, he earned a master's degree in College Student Services Administration at Oregon State University. For more than three decades, he lived in Arizona and worked in higher education, most recently as e-advisor for Phoenix College. In 2014, he retired to the wild Western Slope of Colorado where he lives in the small town of Cedaredge. In his spare time, he draws cartoons and fishes and hikes in the surrounding wilderness.

In addition to writing *A Surface Creek Christmas*, he is the author of *The Four Corners Mystery Series* and *The Great Land Fantasy Series*. Recently married, he and his wife, Donna Marie, have founded **Elevation Press**, a service which helps independent authors design and format books for self-publication. The couple offers free consultation to authors and they welcome new projects. To learn more about the many services offered by **Elevation Press**, please see the final page of this book.

Email: elevationpressbooks@gmail.com
Studio Phone: 970-856-9891
Mail: D.P. Benjamin, P.O. Box 603, Cedaredge, CO 81413
Website: https://benjaminauthor.com/
Visit the Author's Facebook Page under: D.P. Benjamin Author
Instagram: https://www.instagram.com/benjaminnovelist/

The Four Corners Mystery Series by D.P. Benjamin	*The Great Land Fantasy Series* by D.P. Benjamin
• Book 1: *The Road to Lavender*	• Book 1: *Stone Bride*
• Book 2: *A Lavender Wedding*	• Book 2: *Iron Angel*
• Book 3: *Spirits of Grand Lake*	• Book 3: *Redhackle*
• Book 4: *The War Nickel*	• Book 4: *Bindbuilder*
• Book 5: *Rare Earth*	• Book 5: *Nachtfalke*
• Book 6: *Walking Horse Ranch*	• Book 6: *Isochronuous*
• Book 7: *Lavender Farewell*	• Book 7: *Ruth and Esau*

In paperback or Kindle on **amazon.com** and **barnesandnoble.com**.

www.ingramcontent.com/pod-product-compliance
Lightning Source LLC
Chambersburg PA
CBHW060811050426
42449CB00008B/1630